Wielding the Force: The Science of Social Justice

Zainab Amadahy

DEDICATION

This book is dedicated to all the who teach, mentor,
role model and otherwise keep the wisdoms alive.

CONTENTS

ACKNOWLEDGMENTS

Heartfelt and sincere thanks to:

My three sons, Ramon, Leith and Liam who have, in their own unique and distinct ways, been the greatest teachers of my life;

The many Elders who supported my spiritual development: Pauline Shirt, Lee Maracle, Bob Lovelace, Dan Smoke, Mary Lou Smoke and many, many more,

Cover Designer Shandra Spears;

Copy Editor Kateri Akiwenzie-Damm;

Artist Leith Martin, responsible for the interior illustrations;

Judy Rebick and Bob Lovelace for the Forewords, advice and wisdom;

All those who survived genocide, enslavement, war and many other oppressions.

Those that did not survive and need to be remembered and honoured for their contribution to our lives;

My ancestors, descendants and current family – wherever and whenever you are, you contribute to my ongoing spiritual growth;

The many scientists, writers and wise people whose work informed this book;

My readers, fans and critics, without whom my writings would not develop;

All those who struggle for social justice.

***

Many thanks to the Ontario Arts Council that provided funding to support the writing of this book.

i

FOREWORD ONE

On a chilly rainy afternoon in May of 1977 I stood in line along with millions of other people, drawn to theatres by their children, to watch what at first appeared to be a space western. I can't say it was the only cult that my children were exposed to but, thankfully, it has been the most enduring. Having been reared on classic westerns, that afternoon, sitting in the dark flickering world of images and surrounded by the younger generation, I recognized the old narratives: the good guys, the bad guys, the asymmetrical conflict, the love triangle, and on and on. There were also the mystic warriors with their "spiritual force" that shifted the odds just so much as to give the underdogs the possibility of a fighting chance. As we left the theatre on Rideau Street in the rain I wanted tell my boys about the many afternoons I had spent at their age watching black-and-white serial westerns, each week with another wild chase and ending in a "cliffhanger", only to resume the following week with a quick rescue. As I reminisced both boys stopped me and defiantly proclaimed that *Star Wars* was different; different because it had nothing to do with cowboys and Indians. It was in space in a distant galaxy far, far away; a long time ago, or maybe in the future, but there was going to be a series of more movies. Well, I couldn't argue with them. History would have proven me wrong.

When I began to read the final draft of *Wielding The Force: The Science of Social Justice* I have to admit that my hackles were up. I have known Zainab Amadahy for a lot of years. I know her character. Or at least I know her well enough. I knew she saw things well. I didn't think she would take *Star Wars* seriously, really. How could she take the resolute and revolutionary ideas that she lives and breathes and equate them to a "story" recently bought by the Disney Corporation? Well, I would read it as a friend and when we next had time to share a conversation around the kitchen table I would ask her as politely as possible what possessed her to imagine how such a cheap and farcical fantasy could exemplify the poignant and life giving principles she desired to share with the world. I took it personally and why shouldn't I? I share the fight for a better world through peace, cooperation and resistance. I saw my own acquiescence to listening to the CBC in what she had done.

So, history proves me wrong again. It didn't take long while reading *Wielding the Force* that I understood: This book is not about *Star Wars*. It is about compassion. Well, in some ways it is about *Star Wars*. At least in the way that *Star Wars* is about life and struggle and resistance; about asymmetrical conflicts in which we find ourselves oppressed or in league with the oppressed. This is clearly where Zainab positions herself, where I have always found her. This is why this book is legitimate.

More importantly than convincing someone of my age that compassion is "the force", *Wielding* speaks directly to that generation who were convinced as children, and to all of those young hearts and minds who would follow, that the evil empire could be challenged and for that matter overthrown. But like any good story, real life conviction has its challenges. My children's generation has certainly experienced that. Frankly it was easy to take on the trappings of the white cowboy hat or the Jedi master or the mystic warrior from the comfort of a successful middleclass backbench. Worse than a 'rebel without a cause', my generation had more causes to safely tilt our ideals against, and very few real rebels. Our children have become witness to the decline of democracy, challenged by deflation in the value of their labour and so burdened by the cost of climbing the ladder that the rungs literally break under their weight. Brains are filled with uniform half-truths to where personalities within the ranks are indistinguishable. Have you ever wondered why the beings, which had human characteristics in *Star Wars*, were outcasts or the remnants of some indigenous race or species? That's where the force comes in. The force is what challenges synthetic culture. It is the unseen that inhabits the material creation, as surely as the stones, water and air, and quickens life like the fire within us. And in the cold cell of contemporary reflection it may be the only weapon against an increasingly de-humanized society.

Zainab takes the time in her book to speak within the language of contemporary judgment; that is she seeks to explain how science has inadvertently revealed truths about human life that only the mystics once understood. Like the conductor of a sweat lodge she unites the truly simple with the universal and universally complex to explain how the "magic" works. Science is a language within a paradigm, the "world" of progress, manifest destiny, racial superiority, authority and dominion. Whether we are rulers or slaves, science explains us. But like in *Star Wars*, the empire we live within and *the* Empire are inverse realities where everything and everyone is captive. Even science, a powerful source of inquiry is prisoner to unnatural and unsustainable selfishness. The fact that science and those who practice it can challenge the authority of objectivism is evidence that it is subject to the force of compassion. The fact that Zainab uses science as proof that compassion forms a cornerstone of freedom is uncompromising. She has recognized for us that the jailer is also a slave

4

and seeks freedom. It is never the tool that has intention but the conviction of those who would wield the tool that determines its course. The proof is not only in the examples that Science provides but also in the assertion itself. Telling the truth exemplifies courage even in the face of old skeptics like myself.

The heart of *Wielding The Force* is the human heart and all that radiates from its centre. That which holds humanity together is not our sameness but our willingness and ability to accept our differences. Compassion brings these forces into comprehension. It is a force of mindfulness and magic that adds up one and one and makes quintillion or at least what is beyond rational objectivity. For those of us who confront and are confronted by mindless cruelty and oppressive behaviour, and who sometimes hide ourselves in mindless abstractions, Zainab has given us a medicine. Like all good medicine we don't necessarily need to know how it works, just that it does. And like all good healers, Zainab doesn't do the healing; she just knows where to find it. Rather than sorting through an inventory of possibilities *Wielding The Force* reveals the source on which all of the other possibilities rest. The force is within you. It was born with you. It has followed your ancestors across time and when they have used it they have done well. That is why you are here today.

My children understand *Star Wars* much better than I do. *Wielding The Force* will help us all understand it better. I am actually beginning to warm up to it. Although I will never quite accept that it is more entertaining than those old Saturday afternoon serials, I am okay with it. I do know that none of these modern stories will ever hold up to those that Nokomis told when the winter closed in. Now those were the ones that scared you deep into your soul. They were the stories that sharpened your curiosity. Those stories made you laugh and cry at the same time. Those were the stories that gave you courage when you woke at night in the darkness after the fire had burned out. It was in listening to these stories that made me crave freedom and understand that freedom could only come to a just world.

I needed the reminder that the Force with which grandma had told those stories was compassion.

✳✳✳

Robert Lovelace is a continuing adjunct lecturer at Queen's University in the Department of Global Development Studies. His academic interests include Indigenous Studies, sustainable development, and re-Indigenizing society and the commons. Robert is a retired Chief of the Ardoch Algonquin First Nation. He lives in the Algonquin highlands at Eel Lake in the Ardoch Algonquin territory where he continues to offer traditional teaching and ceremony. Robert is also an activist in anti-colonial struggles. In 2008, he spent 3½ months as a political prisoner for his part in defending the Ardoch Algonquin First Nation homeland from uranium exploration and mining. He was released on appeal after a groundbreaking decision of the Ontario Court of Appeal found that Aboriginal law is an essential part of Canadian law. Robert continues to study, write and speak on issues regarding "corporate social responsibility" and the effects of the Canadian mining industry on indigenous people in Canada and internationally. He is currently involved with the "Freedom Flotilla" movement to challenge the illegal blockade of Palestine. Robert also works with an international effort to protect the Great Lakes watershed. His work highlights the intersection between Canadian Indian policy and International reluctance to challenge economic imperialism affecting indigenous peoples around the world.

FOREWORD TWO

Most of my life I have thought of myself, and perhaps been thought of, as a tough activist. It is a reputation that has stood me in good stead especially in polarized battles like the fight for abortion rights. I was fierce and angry much of the time in that battle during the 1980's. Sometimes when I see a clip of myself leading a pro-choice demonstration in front of the Ontario Legislature, I feel afraid. I look so angry. My anger was righteous. The anti-choice movement wanted to impose their religious views on the rest of us, wanted women barefoot, pregnant and in the kitchen and a few of them wanted Dr. Morgentaler and me dead. I had every reason to be angry; although I admit now that my anger came from elsewhere, old wounds that I hadn't yet healed. I put my anger to good use, I guess, but still it had a negative impact.

The first time I realized that my full coat of armour was deleterious to my political work was when I became President of the National Action Committee on the Status of Women in 1990. What made me successful in the battle against the anti-choice and the government made other women, especially marginalized, women uncomfortable, perhaps even frightened. It has taken me 20 years to sort it out and I can still fall back into my old ways, when provoked. I learned a lot from Indigenous women at NAC and later from friends who have studied Buddhism or other practices of love and compassion. I have come to understand that our holier than thou anger hurts the struggle for social change. Our perpetual anger and outrage scares away a lot of people who might otherwise agree with our values and vision. Of course it is hard to restrict anger to those who oppose you. Inevitably it turns against comrades as well. Being an activist is not easy but the hardest part is the brutality we often suffer inside our movements. Brutality is a harsh word I know but I apply it both to the brutality of overwork and overstress as well as the brutality of exaggerated and unnecessarily polarized differences.

Before the G20, I wrote a polemic against black bloc tactics in Vancouver during the Olympics. I knew that people would use these tactics during the G20 too and I wanted to start a debate. But instead of debate, my blog post started a virtual war. I didn't attack anyone personally but I generalized too much not appreciating that many people who use or support black bloc tactics also do work that is very valuable. Instead of a balanced critique, it was an attack and people who support black bloc tactics attacked me in return, some of it quite personal. The best defense is a good offense, the general wisdom of our war metaphors tells us. The effect was to put a chill on the debate, the opposite of the impact I had hoped to have. After all, many people felt, if they can attack Judy Rebick like that, what will they do to me? So they stayed silent and we didn't have the debate. The movement was split and the result was catastrophic, in my view, with 1,100 people arrested and many brutalized. We came together after the arrests and managed to turn public opinion against the police but a lot of people suffered including me. If I had approached my polemic with more compassion, I might have made the same arguments but I would have done so acknowledging the positive contribution that many comrades who support these tactics give to building the movement. I think that would have made all the difference.

It is also that I have come to understand what African American feminist and lesbian activist Audre Lorde said so many years ago, "The Master's tools will never dismantle the Master's house." War is the tool of the Master as is greed, fear and hatred. We have to look elsewhere for our motivations.

In her remarkable book, Wielding *The Force: The Science of Social Justice* Zainab Amadahy makes an extraordinary contribution by proving through her own experience, Indigenous knowledges and science that we need to work from compassion and empathy to achieve the world we want. It is a brave book because it takes head on the argument that our anger is righteous and useful. Yes, she answers it can be if we let it go but not if it becomes who we are and not if it turns into hatred. It is a wise book because it explores all sources of knowledge to make the argument that it is compassion and empathy that must be our driving force not anger and hatred. And it is a humble book because she acknowledges her own limits. She provides a model never assuming that she is right and everyone else is wrong.

But for me the most important part of the book is her argument that relationship building is at the centre of changing the world, not policy, not tactics, not strategies but relationships that have to be at the centre of movement building. It is a profoundly feminist book that takes the women's movement the next step to understand the profound need for, as bell hooks tells us, more love and nurturing in our world and in our movements.

And she points out that it is not just about self-care, it is about caring for ourselves, but also for our comrades and for our communities as well as the planet.

Finally the writing itself is a model of what Zainab is explaining. It is a polemic, an argument but made with compassion, care and humility, hopefully allowing those who would usually reject such arguments to listen and consider.

I've come to think that the ideas so well explained and defended in Zainab's book are central to our ability to change the world. I hope you will open your mind and your heart when you read this book. We will all be stronger and more effective for it.

***

Judy Rebick is a long-time feminist and social justice activist living in Toronto. She is a writer and was the founding publisher of http://www.rabble.ca. Her latest books are *Transforming Power: From the Personal to the Political* (Penguin 2009) and *Occupy This!*, an e book (Penguin 2012). Judy is on the media panel of Q on CBC radio and is the former Sam Gindin Chair in Social Justice and Democracy at Ryerson University. During the 1990s, Judy was the co-host of a national TV Show on CBC. In the 1980s she helped to lead the fight to legalize abortion in Canada, then went on to be elected President of Canada's largest women's group, leading high profile fights around reproductive rights, employment equity, constitutional reform, and anti-racism. In the last ten years, her focus has been more on global solidarity and online activism. Judy's latest preoccupation has been the absence of any real vision on the Left and the lack of effective strategies for transformation. She sees tremendous hope for a total cultural, economic, social and political transformation globally. Her new book outlines the new directions of transformational change that she sees around the world. She is currently working on a memoir of her life in the 1960s.

PREFACE: A NEW HOPE

Have you ever been involved in one of those discussions where someone challenges whether compassion is an appropriate response to human suffering? They may allege that compassion is a contrived emotion that you call up because of the social payback you get from people who recognize you as a caring person. Or worse, they may claim that people "choose" situations that cause them suffering, that it's part of their growth process, and, therefore, although you may feel sorry for them, the best help you can give is to allow people in pain find their own way out of self-created suffering.

I've had such depressing discussions. Compassion is one component of the socially just world I'm struggling to co-create. Cooperation is another keystone in my vision and I've also had several arguments over the years, sometimes with people in my own family, who believe that competition is what drives social and economic development. In their way of thinking, competition is a healthy and natural part of being human while cooperation, especially in the realm of economics, just doesn't work. Cooperatives and collectives are unfair in their very design because people who work hard are rewarded in the same way as people who work less, they argue.

If you're an activist for social justice you've probably had such conversations too. Like me, you might struggle with the underlying feeling that there may be a shred of truth to these arguments and that the vision you want to create, a world full of compassionate, cooperative people contributing to each other's wellbeing, is an impossible dream.

Well, what if hard science was on your side? What if there were biologists, geneticists and neuroscientists who say that cooperation and compassion are not only healthy for us but that they are wired into our biology? That cooperation and compassion are integral to our survival as well as our social and physical evolution?

New and emerging science seems to be making a strong argument in favour of social justice. Social science, sometimes referred to as "soft" science, has always told us that how we choose to structure our communities and allocate resources not only impacts social and economic progress but also our individual health. Now, the so-called "hard" sciences are saying the same thing. Furthermore, this new information suggests that much of what we believe about how the world functions is not entirely accurate and a paradigm shift is in order.

In this book I'd like to review some recent scientific discoveries and see what the implications are for building healthy, sustainable communities. This includes activist communities because this new information has implications for how social change advocates can be more effective in their work, including role modeling the alternatives we aspire to create. For example, have you ever wanted to join an activist group but the unhealthy interpersonal dynamics stopped you? Have you ever participated in an action where someone (or many someones) worked themselves into such a state of rage that they violated group agreements around how the action was to be conducted? In doing so, they may have endangered people's safety and yet continued despite the risk they imposed on others. Have you ever worked in a community organization where colleagues who are theoretically as concerned for the welfare of the world as you are, treat each other and community members with disrespect and disdain?

As activists, many of us have either witnessed or experienced these situations but tend to believe that, for the most part, we understand how they occur. We've built an elaborate analysis around understanding how anti-social behaviours develop. How it's healthy and even desirable to feel anger, frustration and fear in the face of injustice. Basically, we note that unhealthy societies produce unhealthy people. We aren't taught how to cooperate; we're taught how to compete. We aren't taught how to resolve conflicts, we're taught to win them. We aren't taught to embrace difference, we're taught to fear it. We also aren't instructed on how to maintain an awareness of our feelings and manage them. As a result, many people around us, some with considerable wealth and power, role model suppression, denial and/or inappropriate ways of dealing with emotions.

Those of us from marginalized communities (racialized, impoverished, differently-abled, etc.) have been hated, feared and mistreated our whole lives. So of course we're frustrated and angry. That doesn't just turn off because we become activists for social justice or community workers in a non-profit. We self-righteously claim that our anger fuels our activism and desire for change. We're entitled to our anger, we tell ourselves, especially since we channel it into doing social justice work. Meanwhile, racialized people suffer disproportionately from high blood pressure, high rates of cardio vascular disease and other physical symptoms of the injustices we confront on a daily basis[1] and there is reason

[1] Nestyl PhD, Cheryl. Colour Coded Health Care: The Impact of Race and Racism

to believe that our endemic anger is contributing to our unwellness.

We activists understand how unhealthy behaviours impact our work. At best they drain our time and energy. At worst they make it difficult to attract new folks into our movements and burn out our best people. Anti-social behavours can, and do, kill groups. They also kill people, as we very well know. Such behaviours clearly present barriers to achieving our social justice goals.

Activists, to our credit, are able to share beautiful visions of the communities we are working hard to establish. We've created a variety of resources and trainings devoted to helping each other develop cooperative, consensus-building and peace-making skills. Sometimes they work. Other times, not so much. We urge each other to engage in self-care but don't usually consider it an essential part of our activist work, even though we recognize that healthy individuals contribute to the wellness of communities. And we all know that no amount of skills and resources will replace the fundamental desire to work with integrity, honesty and respect.

It's this fundamental desire that this book addresses. *Wielding The Force* will provide you with a new take on old wisdom to inform and reinforce your work for social justice. After reading this book, you will be empowered with persuasive hard science data that can be interpreted and applied using the wisdom you already possess. You will be better able to help people transform their hearts and minds - in that order – because, as the science shows us, emotions play a crucial role in our decision-making and thought processes.

I have written this book because it is my desire that people equate the word *activism* with peace, fairness and kindness. I want activists to be understood as grounded, compassionate and hopeful individuals. The model of activism I espouse is one that literally uses the heart's intelligence, a concept which you will understand as you read on. Information in the following chapters will enable you to ground your activism in a sense of peace and optimism that contributes to personal and collective wellbeing, thus setting the stage for the coming revolutionary shift.

Allow me to illustrate with a story.

Have you ever heard of Matthieu Ricard? If so, you might recall that this French Buddhist monk, renowned for his generosity and kindness, who also has a PhD in molecular genetics, has been dubbed by media as "the happiest man in the world." How could anyone possibly conclude that? Well, today we can identify happiness and other emotions through new technologies that allow us to detect and quantify electrical activity going on in different parts of our brains. Our heart rates and biochemistry can also reveal our emotional states.

---

on Canadians' Health, Wellesley Institute, January 12, 2012.

In 2007 Mattheiu Ricard was a participant in an experiment that aimed to study what was going on in the brains of people who were experiencing a feeling they called "happiness." As it turns out, happiness lights up the pre-frontal cortex with increased synaptic (bio-electrical and chemical) activity that signals all kinds of changes in your biochemistry, in your heart rate and at the molecular level in every cell of your body. Those changes both result from and intensify feelings of wellness and a sense of profound peace, which is one definition of happiness used in such studies. Such changes are also signs of the best states of physical health.

Matthieu Ricard registered more activity in his happy brain than others participating in the study. Researchers, who were amazed at the readings he'd generated, asked the monk what he had been thinking about during the scan. Mr. Ricard answered that he had been meditating on … wait for it … *compassion*! The researchers were surprised. Compassion is not generally seen in our society as a cause of joy. And, while people in good health tend to be joyful, joy hasn't, in and of itself, been understood as an emotion that *creates* physical wellbeing.

Nevertheless, just as emotions like depression, anger and fear generate a physical stress response that jeopardizes health, it has become clear that feelings of compassion, appreciation and gratitude improve health and wellbeing. In fact, deliberately calling up such feelings for a mere five minutes results in five hours of heightened immunity and lowered stress levels.

One of the discoveries that activists particularly like about compassion is that a part of the brain that becomes active when feeling this emotion is the area responsible for planning action. Apparently feeling compassion, that is feeling that you want to alleviate someone's suffering, involves an action component. So the Dalai Lama quote that often appears on my Facebook page, "It is not enough to be compassionate. You must act," has some scientific credibility. Vietnamese Buddhist activist Thich Nhat Hahn was right when he said, "Compassion is a verb."[2]

New and emerging science is further demonstrating that the wellbeing of communities is also enhanced in measurable ways when compassion, cooperation and social justice characterize our relationships. This is contrary to many contemporary worldviews that uphold individualism, competition and the profit motive as the driving forces behind economic progress, social evolution and community wellbeing.

In the succeeding chapters, this book will take a plain language look at how "hard" sciences such as epigenetics and neuroplasticity not only strengthen the argument for social justice but also indicate that a major paradigm shift for all of society is in order. By examining the works of

---

[2] http://www.goodreads.com/author/quotes/9074.Thich_Nhat_Hanh

scientists such as biologist Dr. Bruce Lipton, neuroscientist Dr. Alvaro Pascual-Leone and physicist Dr. Geoffrey West, as well as the work of the HeartMath Institute, the Good Science Centre and the Institute of Noetic Sciences, I will discuss how recent scientific discoveries have major implications for how we understand and co-create healthy relationships, community-building and sustainable activism.

This information will be contrasted and framed within what I'm calling a "relational" worldview, which I will explain and explore. I will further make the case that this framework best allows us to understand and make use of the science; indeed, it is where the science is leading us. I draw a lot on First Nations teachings because it is what I know best, however, I am not suggesting that this knowledge tradition is the only wisdom tradition that exemplifies relational ways of knowing. There are many relational wisdom traditions. I will not be sharing ceremonial knowledge or proselytizing around specific beliefs and practices. What I share of Indigenous North American and other wisdoms will be what is already publicly accessible through various sources, such as films, the worldwide web, and publications.

Similarly, this book will not focus on the history of colonization or attempt to argue that the settler colonial project in North America and other parts of the world is ongoing. If needed, the curious reader and serious activist will find many resources devoted to this topic elsewhere. You can start with CBC's documentary series *8th Fire*[3] and the Defenders of the Land website.[4] In any case, my purpose is not to examine or reveal the many historical and current injustices that exist in our society and around the world but to proceed with the assumption that colonialism and other systemic injustices exist and that the reader has a critical understanding of how these function and to whose benefit.

Furthermore, while I draw on Indigenous cultural knowledge to explore relational paradigms, my purpose in writing this book is not about conversion to any particular political philosophy or spiritual tradition. Although I happen to identify as an Indigenist, I have no interest in colonizing anyone else's thinking in this regard. After all, my own beliefs have shifted and changed over time and will continue to do so. Consequently, I hold no illusions about assuming that my current beliefs are superior to any others. Nor am I convinced they represent some ultimate unshakable truth that will bring wisdom, joy and peace to everyone. Each of us has our own path to follow and our own destination at which to arrive.

---

[3] http://www.cbc.ca/doczone/8thfire/2012/01/wab-kinews-walk-through-history.html
[4] http://www.defendersoftheland.org/

My intent with this book is to share information that we can collectively develop for our common benefit in the interest of improving the quality of life on planet Earth. My hope is that when you read *Wielding The Force* you will be better enabled to make changes in your life, groups and communities that promote wellbeing and social justice.

What is social justice? I can't give a one-size-fits all definition of the term, though I share some thoughts in the final chapter. Each of us must decide what social justice looks like in our own lives. Each of us must further decide whether we consider ourselves to be activists. From my perspective, mothers raising their children to be caring, compassionate and kind may call themselves activists just as much as protesters marching in the streets. First Nations Elders who teach language and culture are activists just as much as those who block roads to prevent uranium mining. Those who demonstrate to city folk how to grow organic vegetables in community gardens are activists just as much as those who stage sit-ins at government offices to advance their demands. The reasons why I believe this will become clear as you read on. Personally, I identify as an activist because I've been committed for years to social justice and wellbeing for myself as well as all other life on the planet. I've struggled as a mom, artist and community worker to rationally argue that caring and sharing make sense in terms of ensuring the survival and flourishing of the human species.

People who believe in "survival of the fittest" as well as the idea that competition and conflict drive innovation and creativity have dismissed my set of beliefs as unsubstantiated and, therefore, unworthy of consideration. Or, as the likes of Immanuel Kant, Ayn Rand and some other highly regarded philosophers might say, the perspective of a 'weak-minded woman driven by emotion'. Consequently, I am greatly excited that, in the course of researching speculative fiction story ideas, I accidentally stumbled upon evidence that my "POV" is actually well-substantiated in new and emerging (though under-publicized) scientific findings. I'm gratified to confirm that my Indigenous teachers, mentors and role models are wiser than many give them credit for as this new hard science knowledge validates cultural practices from First Nations (and many other wisdom) traditions as contributors to community and individual wellbeing. Or as my activist colleagues say, perhaps I should be grateful that the science is catching up to our age-old wisdom.

When viewed through the "relational" lens of some wisdom traditions, new science lays the groundwork for feelings of fulfillment and a sense of purpose that many scientists now consider to be more important to health and happiness than what some people believe makes them happy, such as accumulating wealth, being consistently entertained or getting laid. Not that you can't enjoy these things but it's our relationship to life with all its ups and downs that determines our overall sense of joy and contentment

15

– which in turn impacts our individual and collective wellbeing. The next two chapters are devoted to exploring "relationality" so don't worry if you aren't sure what that means right now.

This book is divided into nine chapters:

➤ **Chapter One: Sith versus Jedi** looks at the question of paradigms, worldviews and ideologies – frameworks that help us make sense of our world. This chapter contrasts some key features of the dominant cultural paradigm as well as leftist paradigms, with those of global Indigenous peoples. This is to generate understanding of and appreciation for indigenous and other relational ways of knowing, which have much to offer advocates of social justice.

➤ **Chapter Two: Spidey Forces** goes further in depth to explore the concept of "relationality" to enable the reader to grasp some fundamental differences between leftist knowledge paradigms and those of Indigenous and other wisdom traditions. It will further examine intersections and compatibility among paradigms as well as demonstrate the advantages of sharing and interacting across knowledge traditions.

➤ In **Chapter Three: My Adventures in the Jedi Academy of Life**, I preface sharing my story of being an activist with a look at the issue of social location and how it might matter to the discussions the book provokes.

➤ **Chapter Four: The Internal Force** deals with new hard science discoveries around the mind/body connection and discusses the implications for social change.

➤ **Chapter Five: Jedi Heart Tricks** examines the role of the heart organ in the mind/body connection and its relevance to the struggle for social justice. Practical exercises in the chapter demonstrate this connection to readers.

➤ **Chapter Six: Jedi Brain Tricks** looks at the implications of recent discoveries in brain science and their relevance to activism and social change.

➤ **Chapter Seven: Intersecting Force Fields** explores findings about the science of relationships and interactions; our energetic connections to other life forms on the planet and the planet Herself, as well as to each other, again teasing out the relevancy for social justice advocates. This will be the longest chapter in the book because it's the meat of what concerns me: the science of human interactions.

➤ **Chapter Eight: Shape-Shifting Tricksters** focuses on the critiques, concerns and limitations of the above information as it applies to social justice activism.

> ➤ **Chapter Nine: Activist Forces** answers the question, "Now that we have this information, how do we effectively apply it in our social justice work?" This chapter argues that emerging science is informing a paradigm shift that can and should support the transformation to social justice. Armed with this new information activists can hasten our collective transition to a kinder, healthier world.

I hope that, though we may disagree on some details you will emerge from this book transformed and better able to contribute to co-creating a new, wondrous and rEVOLutionary world. Our collective paradigm is shifting and science is firmly on the side of social justice! Like the rebels of the original Star Wars trilogy who brought down the evil Empire, activists can effectively wield "The Force."

CHAPTER ONE: SITH VERSUS JEDI

As someone who was raised in the Christian tradition, later became an atheist and now identifies as a spiritual person, I struggle everyday with understanding the "relational" framework that informs how Indigenous peoples and others both sense and make sense of our world. Paradigms and worldviews are important in terms of how we collect, interpret and apply information. They are crucial to formulating a sense of curiosity. Before we get into how worldview impacts our understanding of emerging science and how that knowledge informs the struggle for social justice, we need to explore the question of paradigms. Before that, I will explain what I mean by terms like *worldview* and *paradigm*. That's tough because our paradigms and worldviews are so engrained and normalized that often we aren't aware that we have them, much less are able to define them. It might be a bit like describing colour to someone who is colour blind. Or like someone who is visually impaired explaining to a sighted person how s/he navigates through the world. Often it is not until we are confronted with a different paradigm that we can comprehend both the opportunities and limitations of our own way of thinking.

My middle son was (and is) a speculative fiction writer and as a child he used to enjoy musing about how life forms that evolved in other parts of the universe might look, think and act. He used creatures that had evolved on Earth to stimulate his imagination. How might a bat, he once asked, which is almost blind and depends on echolocation, "see" the world? How would the bat's way of seeing affect its way of thinking?

Human beings have only three colour receptors. This enables us to see the spectrum of colours that make up the rainbow. But our visual range does not allow us to see *all* the colours produced by a rainbow. Butterflies have at least five colour receptors, which means they can see colours well outside of our visual range. Sparrows have the capacity to see in the ultraviolet and infrared ranges, so they see colours at both ends of the rainbow. The preying mantis shrimp, which lives in the shallow waters of coral reefs, has *16 colour receptors*! They can see colours beyond our imagination! If we could wear glasses that allowed us to see what a preying

18

mantis shrimp does, it would change our view of the world in ways we cannot currently comprehend. So it is with paradigms and worldviews. At the risk of not being well understood just yet, I am going to describe worldview as the filter through which we sense, interpret and understand our reality. For the purposes of this book the words *worldview* and *paradigm* are synonymous. A worldview is a set of beliefs that helps us make sense of the information we receive through our senses. This paradigm enables us to give meaning to and connect our life experiences. Our worldview sometimes gives us a feeling of security as it allows some predictability into our lives. That way we can safely make future plans. For example, one worldview may have you predict that your headache will end in a few minutes because you've swallowed a pill. Another worldview would have you predict the end of your headache because you've participated in a healing ceremony.

Paradigms come with a set of values; that is, a group of ideas that are considered important; ways of being that everyone is urged to see as, "normal," "natural," or simply inherent to life. For instance, in the dominant worldview of North America, competition is something that is valued. Most people believe that being competitive is not only normal and natural but desirable. Competition plays a beneficial role in spawning technological achievements that make life easier, some believe. It also keeps the price of consumer goods low so that we can all enjoy those achievements equally. Competition is responsible for human existence according to Darwinist theories of evolution, wherein two-leggeds are considered the winners of the survival-of-the-fittest contest.

In this worldview, we lose our motivation to do better in the absence of competition. Without competition people don't perform well. For instance, Leonard Sax, M.D and PhD., believes that males in particular are motivated by the desire to win. Thus, providing a competitive environment in classrooms and in other aspects of life enables the male of the species to better contribute to society.[5]

In another example, Canadians decried the lack of competition in phone services some 30+ years ago when Bell had a monopoly in North America. Consumer groups and other phone service providers advocated for laws that created a competitive environment for communications services so the Canadian government deregulated the industry between 1980-97, breaking Bell's monopoly. Whether this ultimately resulted in reduced prices for consumers and greater technological innovation is a matter for debate. And some ask whether the question is actually relevant to our quality of life.

---

[5] Sax, Leonard. *Boys Adrift: The Five Factors Driving the Growing Epidemic of Unmotivated Boys and Underachieving Young Men*, Basic Books. 2008.

Indigenous people might point out (I among them) that European beliefs about the value of competition were used in North America to rationalize the seizing by European settlers of what were once collectively stewarded lands. First Peoples and their cultures were characterized as inferior in part due to the fact that we did not relate to land and resources in a competitive fashion; that is, most of our communities weren't organized around accumulating material wealth. The different ways First Nations and European peoples related (and in many cases, still relate) to land is based in differing worldviews; different ways of thinking.

An easy, introductory way that most of us can understand the idea of paradigm or worldview is to study how the right and left sides of the human brain deal with information. If you Google "right brain, left brain" you will find many websites that explain how the different hemispheres of your brain function. Because the information is so readily available, I'll be brief here.

The left side of your brain is logical and rational. It likes hard facts, especially when they're sequential and ordered. If information doesn't come that way it will attempt to organize it accordingly. Your left-brain is linear and generally sees things in terms of their cause and effect. Viruses cause colds, for example, or human beings need to consume specific amounts of food from different food groups in order to stay healthy. The future does not interest your left-brain, which is concerned with the past and present. The left-brain is analytical, methodical and diagnostic. It likes to think of itself as objective in that it can position itself outside of what it senses and observes. It doesn't develop emotional attachments to the data it manages. Your left-brain is concerned with accuracy and interested in how the small parts of something contribute to the functioning of the whole. How do atoms form molecules? How do molecules form cells in our bodies? How do cells affect the way our organs function? Your left brain learns about something from analyzing its parts.

Your right brain, on the other hand, is both intuitive and random. It likes looking at how things relate to each other rather than looking at linear causality. Your right brain sees the world as a spider web, where every strand has a crucial role in the web's function; where your cold might be the result of many factors such as exposure to a virus and low immunity as well as emotional stress; where your experience of being sick might feed life lessons back to you about how to take better care of yourself or the next person in your life who falls ill. The right side of your brain is very subjective and involved in what it senses. It reacts to and is influenced by the information it processes. It's also concerned with aesthetics, emotions and creativity. Your right brain understands something by looking at the big picture; how the whole interacts within a larger system. You are able to fantasize, dream and imagine thanks to your right brain.

In the "Human Brain" graphic you'll see a summary of right and left brain functions. (Graphics in print might be blurry but are crisp and clear on my website: www.swallowsongs.com)

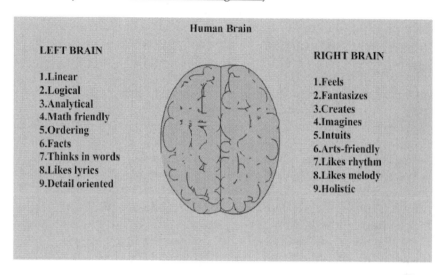

Human Brain

LEFT BRAIN

1.Linear
2.Logical
3.Analytical
4.Math friendly
5.Ordering
6.Facts
7.Thinks in words
8.Likes lyrics
9.Detail oriented

RIGHT BRAIN

1.Feels
2.Fantasizes
3.Creates
4.Imagines
5.Intuits
6.Arts-friendly
7.Likes rhythm
8.Likes melody
9.Holistic

At first glance it's easy to see that the two sides of your brain approach the world from seemingly opposite, conflicting points of view. In most of us, one side of the brain is more dominant than the other, influencing which information we take in, how we take it in and what we do with it. That's partly why some of us make better accountants than nurses, why most artists I know dislike math and why scientists sometimes devalue the contributions of spiritual thinkers. I like to think of the left-brain as the mouse's perspective and the right as the eagle's. Mice have very poor eyesight, which is why they tend to run along the floorboards of a room and hide in corners. These little creatures rely on their sense of hearing, whiskers and sensations on their fur to help them navigate through the world. They react to tangible, concrete objects in their environment. In many instances they don't sense an obstacle in their path until they are literally up against it. Eagles, on the other hand, illustrative of the right brain, have sharp eyesight. They fly higher than all other winged creatures and look down on the world from their vantage point in the sky. They can see brilliant colours and details of vast landscapes and hunt by taking in the big picture, studying the interaction of the life beneath them, while also being able to focus on details from a great distance.

The thing is, both ways of sensing the world, as represented by mice and eagles have their uses, benefits and advantages. Of course, the eagle and the mouse may not closely communicate or cooperate, certainly not in ways as complex as your right and left brain. But the two hemispheres of your brain definitely communicate, cooperate and collaborate on receiving, processing and acting on information. This is called *brain integration*.

Even though one side of the brain may be more influential in your thinking, both sides are involved in the process. Furthermore, integration between the left and right brain impacts your physical health as well as your thinking. We now know the more communication and cooperation between the right and left hemispheres, the more you benefit through better physical health and increased mental capacity. Unfortunately, if you spent your childhood in the North American school system you've probably received an education that valued and strengthened your left-brain skills over your right. You can change this with varying amounts of effort, depending on a number of factors, such as your natural (genetic) inclination, the cultural paradigm in which you function and the activities on which you spend most of your time. It possibly changes with age anyway. For example, scientists have recently found that the brain's language centre starts out in the left hemisphere but by the time we reach our senior years, both hemispheres are heavily involved in processing language.[6] In any case, the point I'm making here is that seeing the world only from one vantage point, leading your life only from the mouse's point of view, for example, has its limitations.

Yet this type of either/or, black or white, thinking is typical of the dominant paradigm. Libertarian author Ayn Rand once said, "There are two sides to every issue, one side is right and the other is wrong, but the middle is always evil."[7] She is also credited with the quote, "Any white person who brings the element of civilization has the right to take over this continent [North America]," which is one outcome of the assumption that all ideas in life have to be put into antagonistic camps. The structure of debates and even the "democratic" system of voting in elections is pretty much based on the either/or, right/wrong principle; either this is true or that is; either she's is the people's choice or he is. Yet we know that very few aspects of life, very little of what actually goes on in the world is either/or. We don't live in a Star Wars universe where everyone must be aligned with either the Sith or the Jedi.

I have come to think of paradigms/worldviews as similar to the pair of glasses I put on to enable me to see well. I wear bi-focals so when I want to see something up close I look through the bottom part of my lenses. If I

---

[6] "Language 'Center' Of Brain Shifts With Age". Science Daily. April 28, 2004. http://www.sciencedaily.com/releases/2004/04/040428062634.htm

[7] http://www.brainyquote.com/quotes/quotes/a/aynrand387290.html

want to see something far away I look through the top. Having access to both of these views generally improves my capacity to see what is in my environment. This is my understanding of how paradigms are useful to us. There are many paradigms and some may be more useful than others in specific situations but when combined they probably all contribute in some way to a more comprehensive understanding of reality. On the other hand, drawing from only one paradigm can deprive you of the advantages and benefits of a more comprehensive worldview. As former Ardoch Algonquin co-Chief, Elder, educator and activist Robert Lovelace has noted, "On their own paradigms do not struggle or, as you would expect, conflict with one another. … Opposition is … an imagined condition and not represented in nature's practice."[8] Nevertheless, it is quite possible that the lenses in your pair of glasses can crack. Damaged lenses prevent us from seeing anything clearly and that is an analogy that could be applied to paradigms that jeopardize the survival of human and other species. We'll discuss this more in the final chapter.

Another way of looking at paradigms might be to think of hiking up a trail to enjoy the vista from a mountaintop. There are probably many paths leading up to the top of the mountain. Some might meander while others are straight. Some might be overgrown with bush and studded with sharp rocks while others are clear and easy to tread. Each path provides you with a different experience of your journey.

In going up the mountain you might start on one path and decide to switch to another. You might decide to take your time and enjoy the vistas or stride quickly, to the top. Your reasons for climbing, (getting fresh air and exercise, spending quality time with loved ones, guiding a bunch of tourists from the city, etc.) will influence your experience of the climb. When you reach the top you'll enjoy pretty much the same view as anyone else who makes it up there with you. At the same time, your feelings about making it to the top might depend on your reasons for embarking on the journey and your experience of the journey itself. Furthermore, those feelings around your experience very much inform what you see and the importance you assign to it, as we'll discuss later. My point is there are many legitimate ways to get to the mountaintop and many legitimate and understandable feelings about arriving there. Feelings concerning what to value about the journey and the destination are going to vary from person to person. Furthermore, there are many mountaintops from which to enjoy the view. When you get to the top you might see someone on a mountain opposite yours, looking down into the same valley as you, but seeing it all

---

[8] Lovelace, Robert. "Foretelling the Future: Philosophical Discussions of Witchcraft and Culture" Lecture Notes. Used with permission. Former Co-Chief of the Ardoch Algonquin First Nation is an Elder, educator, author and activist.

very differently. If you were to compare notes on what you saw later you might find they saw things you didn't and vice versa. Just because from your vantage point you couldn't see what they saw doesn't mean it wasn't there.

My point here is that your framework may allow you to see some things but block you from seeing others. It may leave you frustrated that people who operate within a different worldview don't see what you do or can't understand the importance you may attach to what you see.

In this way relationality, as the cornerstone of Indigenous and other wisdoms, is no less valid than Eurocentric worldviews, be they right or left wing. Those of us who see the world through relational glasses just might not share the same reasons as you do for climbing the mountain. You may not choose my path or even my mountain and consequently what you see and your feelings about what you see might be very different from mine. Unfortunately, when one person on the mountaintop has more power than all the others and can coerce people into seeing and doing things her way, it can cause problems. Especially when her way has unhealthy consequences for all.

As in right and left brain integration, clear, frequent and thorough communication as well as developing equitable and just relationships across our cultural paradigms, enables us to gain insight into each other's mindsets and get a more comprehensive idea of what's really going on in our world. It enables us to share solutions to problems or move forward in a way that avoids problems. We may never fully understand each other but we can appreciate, respect and value what each of us has to offer to complete the big picture.

Now I realize that to many social justice activists discussion of paradigms is often about right and left wing philosophies - capitalism versus socialism versus anarchy, for example. What I'm advocating might go against Eurocentric leftist political and social theories that see right and left paradigms as oppositional and contradictory; that see conflict, specifically class conflict, and not relationality as the driving force of social change.

Unfortunately, these theories are as foreign to Indigenous relational ways of knowing as those of liberal democrats, libertarians and capitalists. Anishinaabeg scholar and activist Leanne Simpson points out that...

> Western theory, whether based in post-colonial, critical or even liberatory strains of thought, has been exceptional at diagnosing, revealing and even interrogating colonialism; and many would argue that this body of theory holds the greatest promise for shifting the Canadian politic because it speaks to that audience in a language they can understand, if not hear. Yet western theories of

liberation have for the most part failed to resonate with the vast majority of Indigenous Peoples, scholars or artists. In particular, western-based social movement theory has failed to recognize the broader contextualizations of resistance within Indigenous thought, while also ignoring the contestation of colonialism as a starting point.[9]

Simpson has indicated that she's more interested in exploring Indigenous theories and teachings because they speak to Indigenous peoples, valuing and embodying our knowledge ways. I would further argue that leftist theory, for the most part, still has difficulty embracing, comprehending and coming to terms with relational paradigms. In fact, it too can be quite reductionist, linear and materialist in its orientation. And while we who function within relational worldviews can and do incorporate reductionism, linearity and materialism into our story of how the world functions (though these will never dominate our thinking), I don't believe that the reverse is true. At least not yet.

In any case, it's not right or left wing philosophies that I am addressing when I juxtapose worldviews/paradigms in this book. It is the paradigms of materialism versus energy or "relationality" that I want to explore. Quantum physics has been attempting to resolve these paradigms for at least half a century. The discovery that light can behave as either matter or energy kicked off a continuing discussion about whether our universe is partly comprised of particles of matter or whether everything we sense in our reality is actually, at its core, energy.

Materialism is the notion that what we term *matter* is actually made up of microscopic particles: molecules formed by atoms, formed by sub atomic particles and on down. Science is always thinking it has found the smallest particle of which matter is comprised, only to have a new discovery that there is something smaller. Mainstream science likes to look at how these particles function, interact and lend properties to the materials that they make up. This is a significant difference in Eurocentric and Indigenous thinking and this has implications for how we relate to each other and the Earth we share. Professor of American Studies John Mohawk (Seneca) illustrates this below:

> Let's say you have three people approach a tree.
> One's a socialist materialist, one's a capitalist

---

[9] Simpson, Leanne. Dancing on our Tuttle's Back: Stories of Nishnaabeg Re-Creation, Resurgence and a New Emergence. Arbeiter Ring Publishing, 2011. P. 31.

materialist and one's a traditional native person. The capitalist materialist will explain to you that he has to cut the tree down because this is the best interest not only of himself but also of society; that it is a kind of destiny; that by cutting the tree down he will rationally distribute the materials from the tree and he'll do the most good for the people. A socialist person approaching the tree will also tell you to cut the tree down, because after cutting the tree down you can distribute it equally to everybody and it's going to do the most good for the world that way. But a native person looking at the tree will say that the tree, in its unharmed, original form, has a value that's greater than anything the others are proposing.[10]

Of course, this is an oversimplification to make a point. Indigenous people have been known to chop down trees and non-Indigneous folks have certainly been known to protect them. But the example does illustrate different ways of thinking about trees and their place in our world.

The world's Indigenous peoples have had difficulty comprehending and accepting materialist paradigms since the time of colonization. From an Indigenous understanding it is energy or Spirit that is at the core of everything we sense in our realm and this is what I believe to be a crucial point of tension between Eurocentric worldviews and those of others. It's not that we don't comprehend or accept that there is a materiality to the world and that "materials" or particles interact in certain consistent and sometimes predictable ways. It's just that we comprehend that the behavior of the material world is governed by Spirit or "life force".

For those who believe relationality, as I've explained it thus far, conflicts with leftist social theory, I make the observation that:

1) Relational worldviews, while emphasizing peace (inner and outer), reciprocity and other values do, in fact, see conflict in some situations as conducive to social change. Tension and conflict are seen as functional in many contexts. That's why so many wise and courageous people block access to roads and otherwise engage in actions that prevent resource exploitation and oppose activities that threaten the survival of human and other life forms. Most of the people I know who engage in these actions make an articulate case that these tactics are employed as a last resort, in

---

[10] Mohawk, John. "Subsistence and Materialism" in Tauli-Corpuz, Victoria & Mander, Jerry, Eds. *Paradigm Wars: Indigenous Peoples' Resistance to Globalization*. Sierra Club Books & University of California Press. 2006. Page 26.

defense of the life we are dependent upon. We'll explore this thinking in more detail in the Spidey Forces Chapter.

2) If we were to apply conflict theories to the human body what we would see is disease and illness. Auto-immune disease, for example, is characterized by cells attacking each other in the body. How well would your body function if the liver declared war on the stomach or the lungs starved the body of oxygen? It's only when the different parts of your body cooperate that you can experience wellness. At the same time, your immune system will attack foreign invaders such as viruses and bacteria that make you sick. Your immune system keeps you alive and functioning to the best of its ability. So there is a role for conflict within the body as well but it's a specific role, useful in specific contexts.

As a social justice advocate I'm sure you can make a convincing case to equate capitalism, colonialism and other "isms" that cause deadly social illnesses with pathogens or auto-immune diseases. At the same time, I've been taught by my Indigenous teachers that we two-leggeds are part of Mother Earth's body. When we harm each other, or harm the survival capacity of the other life that we depend upon to sustain us, the whole system suffers.

I'm not arguing in favour of anyone and everyone adopting an Indigenous paradigm. From what I understand of Buddhism, Sufism and other worldviews these are also relational paradigms; Indigenism is not the only one. I also don't want to suggest that *all* the teachings of these traditions are "correct," "factual" or even useful. I'm simply providing one of many possible ways to help you understand relationality and contrast it with other ideologies that inform social justice activism.

Since we're going to be discussing science it might be helpful to look at a couple of paradigms that govern the formation of scientific questions, data collection and the interpretation of information, as well as how information gets used. See Table I on the following page for a summary of Scientific Paradigms and Table II on page 29 for a quick look at the Role of "Scientists" in both frameworks.

If we look at the prevailing cultural understanding of what science is, what it is not and the role it plays in society we'll find something very similar to the left-brain paradigm. In the dominant culture, science is concerned with measuring and counting. What quantities of medication produce the desired results? How many stress hormones can our body tolerate without negative consequences and for how long? Left-brained science tends to be reductionist in that it looks at how the parts contribute to the whole, sometimes extracting the pieces and separating them out in order to study them, for example, removing organs to dissect them or looking at the behavior of cancer cells under a microscope. Left-brained science tends to be linear in its search for causality. Exploring whether A leads to B leads to C, for instance. How does the breast cancer gene lead to cancer? This science is further concerned with replication and provability. Is there an ordered, sequential set of events in a specific context that cause the same results every single time?

Table I: Scientific Paradigms

Mainstream	Relational
<ul><li>Measures, quantifies</li><li>Linear, looks for causality</li><li>Reductionist: how parts contribute to the whole</li><li>Duplication, provability, empiricism</li><li>Science is separate from art, philosophy, etc. Science has a specific and limited frame of reference.</li></ul>	<ul><li>Cycles, rhythms</li><li>Transformation, change – nothing is static</li><li>Connection, interaction within a complex network</li><li>Holistic, big picture</li><li>Multi-disciplinary: includes philosophy, art, mythology, ceremony & prayer, etc.</li></ul>

In the dominant culture a scientist is a professionally trained person, supposedly an objective observer of the outcome of her research. She often works in a lab but even when she doesn't she must control or at least strive to account for all the variables that might impact her research. Furthermore, she is given the *limited* right to interfere in the natural course of events in her quest for knowledge. For example, she can terminate the life of a non-human for no other reason than to better understand it. She may infect an animal with disease, alter its body surgically or extract genetic material from one life form and inject it into another for the purposes of learning and/or transforming life forms so they better serve perceived human needs.

Ultimately, mainstream science seeks to understand as a precursor to control. If we control our bodies and our environment we will not have to suffer illness, discomfort or even die. In his latest book, theoretical physicist Michio Kaku (USA) predicts that by the year 2100 humans will be "masters of nature" and that "our destiny is to become like the gods we once worshipped and feared."[11] He excitedly declares that in this future, humans will enjoy "perfect" bodies and extended lifetimes; we'll even be able to create life forms that have not previously walked the Earth. Kaku's predictions showcase the logic behind the prevailing scientific worldview.

---

[11] Kaku, Michio. *The Physics of the Future: How Science Will Shape Human Destiny and Our Daily Lives by the Year 2100.* Doubleday. 2011.

The dominant paradigm sees science as a completely different field of knowledge, separate from philosophy, art, religion and others. That is

Table Ii: The Role Of "Scientists"

Mainstream Scientist	Enquirer/Scientist in Relational Worldview
• Objective observer • Controller • Professional, trained • Interferes with nature to learn or cure or … • Collects data in the search for tangible facts& information, so we can exert control over our lives & environments • Questions of wisdom, purpose, etc. are within the realm of psychology, philosophy & religion	• Participant – influences and is influenced by the subject of enquiry; intention matters; feelings matter • Respects, cares for, cooperates with and co-exists with life so life will show and share its gifts • Respects and desires uncontrollability because of its contribution to the ongoing regeneration of life • Searches for meaning, purpose, lessons, wisdom

why many famous scientists, for example, particularly in relation to research around atomic energy, have claimed a sense of innocence and lack of accountability in the development of nuclear weapons. From their point of view they've discovered a tangible fact about the way the universe works and developed a way to manipulate that process. Whether the information is used to harm or serve humankind is not within their realm of scientific responsibility. Standing Rock Sioux activist, scholar and author Vine Deloria notes, "Western civilization, unfortunately, does not link knowledge and morality but rather, it connects knowledge and power and makes them equivalent."[12] In this worldview, science is about enabling human dominance over the universe. In practice so far, it has attempted to enable the dominance of humans over other life forms that share our planet as well as *some* humans over others.

In looking at an example of a relational paradigm, I focus on First Nations "science," although some people question the use of that word to

---

12

http://www.brainyquote.com/quotes/authors/v/vine_deloria_jr.html#RcQLEV XdT8BLUrQA.99

describe Indigenous knowledge ways. Yet, the word "science" comes from the Greek word "knowledge" and all peoples have legitimate, valid knowledge. If Indigenous peoples on Turtle Island (North America) did not have viable knowledge we would not have survived, especially through colonialism and genocide. At the same time I think that the concept of "science" as it is understood in mainstream society is too limiting to apply to Indigenous knowledge ways. Nevertheless, for the sake of contrasting the two paradigms, I'm going to use the word here.

Dr. Gregory Cajete (Tewa) describes science as nothing more than a story about the world and our relationship to it.[13] Indigenous "science" and other relational knowledge paradigms tell a story that is less concerned with measuring and counting than with finding and participating in patterns, cycles and rhythms. The relational worldview understands and accepts that transformation and change are ongoing in all aspects of life. Nothing stays the same or remains still. Everything shifts, moves and undergoes complete makeovers. Birth and death are seen as transformations and not as beginnings and endings. Life shifts into spirit and "material" forms over and over again in never-ending cycles. Our long gone ancestors and those of generations yet to be born are beings with whom we interact. The more we two-leggeds align ourselves with the rhythms and cycles of the natural world, co-existing in harmonious ways with other life forms and the planet Herself, the more knowledge is revealed to us *and* the more wisdom we develop to guide its application.

The notion of Spirit, an invisible force that imbues and comprises all life; that governs creation, death and the transformations of all that we know and then some, is fundamental to the relational worldview. Although, certainly not all wisdom traditions use the term "spirit" and translating Indigenous concepts into English is hardly an exact science. However, since I'm not fluent in any Indigenous language and this book is in English we will use the word "spirit" here

As we have discussed, Indigenous people look at how everything and everyone connects to and influences each other through a complex set of relationships. Consequently, attempting to exert control over our world becomes a futile exercise. We can never account for all interactions that impact our reality, and consequently we could never plan and compensate for them. In fact, an ever-changing, constantly shifting environment is desirable because it ensures the ongoing creation, development and regeneration of life. A closed, static system signifies death to the Indigenous mindset. It's the introduction of change, including difficulty, into the mix that generates growth and renewal. You can see this in your

---

[13] Cajete Ph.D., Gregory. *Native Science: Natural Laws of Interdependence.* Clear Light Publishers, 2000, page 27.

own life. Although you may not enjoy challenges that have come your way, it is in managing such challenges that you have gained knowledge, deepened relationships or developed the spiritual "muscles" that allow you to cope better with life. Does a child ever learn to walk without falling? Can athletes excel without pushing through pain? Even the body after death decomposes and contributes to the renewal of life.

In the relational worldview we do not cease to exist in death but transform from a "material" manifestation into an energetic/spiritual one that continues to contribute to the ongoing development and regeneration of life. As Cajete notes, to the mind of the Indigenous scientist "... truth is not a fixed point, but rather an ever-evolving point of balance, perpetually created and perpetually new."[14] The "goal" or desired outcome of Indigenous scientific inquiry is to experience a sense of oneness with the Great Spirit; to feel the joys of being, sharing and contributing to wellness and ongoing creation.

Indigenous knowledge ways are more concerned with the holistic, big picture than its component parts. Spirituality, art, philosophy, ceremony and many other fields of knowledge are connected to, influence and interact with each other. In fact, they aren't even understood as separate fields. Ceremony and art, for instance, are ways in which information can be asked for, received and processed – even created. Indeed, even mainstream science notes that making, engaging in and even appreciating art contributes to physical and cognitive brain development. Different knowledge disciplines cannot be separated any more than one can draw a line between a wave and the ocean that formed it.

Unfortunately, colonial culture denigrates and ridicules Indigenous knowledge. It is frequently dismissed as folk knowledge or folk medicine, of limited value, even though scientists from other cultures are often keen on documenting Indigenous wisdom, patenting it and selling it for profit. The number of White "healers" and New Agers holding dangerous and expensive "sweat lodge ceremonies" is a case in point. Unfortunately, too many people who steal this knowledge don't always get it right and pose a danger to those they work with. One extreme example that made international news in 2009 is that of motivational speaker James Ray whose sweat lodge for a total of 64 people killed three and made 21 ill. The plastics he used in his structure and the processes he used in the "ceremony" bore absolutely no resemblance to any legitimate sweat lodge ceremony and Ray was later convicted on three counts of negligent homicide.

In another example, it was the Anishinaabeg who discovered the healing properties of Essaic tea, which is now manufactured, distributed

---

[14] Cajete, Gregory. 19.

and sold in health food and herbal medicine stores for a profit by various non-Indigenous companies. Those peoples who discovered the healing power of Essaic, cared for the plant and its environment and continue to pass down the information over generations are not compensated for their knowledge or centuries of work.

An Indigenous enquirer (scientist) is also trained, a lifetime of it, but her training might involve ceremonial protocols, the use of sacred medicine items as well as special songs, dances and stories that create the best conditions under which to ask for, receive, process and apply information. The Indigenous "scientist" is a participant in her research, both influencing and being influenced at all stages, from formulating a question to receiving an answer to processing the response and finally to sharing it with her community. This is not a linear or stepped process, however. Professor Cajete in his book *Native Science: Natural Laws of Interdependence* notes that in the Indigenous worldview, spirituality is not a relationship between an individual and God but a much more complex one where the crucial interactions occur between communities and the Great Mystery/Creator. I would say the same is true in the realm of Indigenous "science." The quest for knowledge and the wisdom to use it is one in which the whole community takes part, although individuals may have specific roles to play in the process.

The Indigenous knowledge-seeker cannot conceptually or physically distance herself from what she is studying or questioning. Her lifetime training involves learning about herself as much as her Relations. She needs to appreciate and observe the world in which she is a part as well as how she interacts with it. It is when we respect and take part in the natural world that Our Relations reveal their knowledge and wisdom. Consequently, the Indigenous "scientist" is reluctant to interfere in "natural" processes – the cycles, rhythms and patterns of Creation. Interventions are considered very carefully, within community, where Elders, ancestors and other Spirit Beings have substantial input. This is because the intricate balance of relationships and interconnections that generate and provide for life are respected, valued and understood to be so complex that there could be serious consequences for altering it.

One of the more significant underpinnings of relational knowledge ways is, in contrast to materialism, a concern with energy. The science of the dominant culture is increasingly becoming convinced that if we want to understand more about our world we need to focus less on the particles we keep studying and more on the energies surrounding, governing and, perhaps, comprising them. Increasingly, even mainstream science is coming to understand that it is energy that determines the behaviour of matter in our universe.

Perhaps you remember in grade school doing an experiment where iron shavings were placed on a sheet of paper and a magnet was moved underneath. The magnet determined the behaviour of the iron shavings above, even though there was no direct contact between the shavings and the magnet. This is the way in which my Indigenous teachers understand how prayer and ceremony act in the "material" world.

What is energy? The best definition I've heard is that energy is information. For example, the energy of our feelings, thoughts and intentions, fortified by song, dance, medicines/herbs, ancestor power, and so on, actually influence how our physical bodies and other life forms behave. Physical sensations and thoughts are entangled with emotions. For every feeling we experience, every thought we have, there is a corresponding physical reaction. That's true in reverse as well. We'll see that hard science has made significant inroads to demonstrate this but if you find yourself skeptical at this idea think about stress. It's hardly controversial anymore to recognize that our emotional reactions to events in our lives can impact our bodies, sometimes making us ill. Likewise, injuries and illnesses impact our emotional states.

Mainstream science is catching up to Indigenous knowledge in finding that energy, in its various known forms such as sound, magnetism and electricity as well as thoughts and feelings, determines how matter behaves. One big difference, however, is that mainstream science does not necessarily consider these energies to be infused with consciousness, emotion or intellect. But if science declares our thoughts and feelings to be nothing more than electro-chemical reactions (energetic activity) in the brain, then energy is at least as aware, emotional and intelligent as we humans are.

To the Indigenous scientist, thoughts and feelings matter in the seeking out and application of knowledge. Thoughts and feelings impact results. Furthermore, the Indigenous scientist is not seen as superior to other life forms but related and connected to them. In this tradition, respecting, caring for, cooperating with, and co-existing with other life forms, their transformations, rhythms, and cycles, is what enables us to learn, grow, and transform ourselves. The closer we are to nature, the more we align ourselves with its rhythms and patterns, the more our senses open, heightening our awareness of what is going on around us. We then benefit from a heightened awareness, presence and joy in our experience of being.

Of course these scientific paradigms are generalizations about two polarized knowledge ways and don't speak to the reality that there are exceptions, common understandings and increasing communication across cultures. Both approaches have validity and can sometimes lead us to the same place, as we will later see. However, it's, of course, problematic when one scientific paradigm dominates and is seen as more valid and more valuable than the other. Worse is when one knowledge way is backed up by coercive structures that can support the simultaneous dismissal and theft of knowledge with impunity. Such abuses of power discourage communication and sharing across our cultures. In the end, colonization makes it difficult, if not impossible, to work together to grow our common knowledge for common good. But just as right- and left-brain integration improves mental and physical health, we could choose to work together across our paradigms to improve the quality of life for all beings on planet Earth.

CHAPTER TWO: SPIDEY FORCES

Relational worldviews, expressed in the following paraphrased Cherokee teaching, stress the inter-connectedness and interdependence of all life.

Mother Earth and all her children teach us that diversity is necessary to our health and well-being. You don't see the trees insisting that they all bear the same fruit. You do not see the fish declaring war against those who do not swim. You don't see corn blocking the growth of squash and beans. What one plant puts into the soil, another takes. What one tree puts into the air another creature breathes. What one being leaves as waste another considers food. Even death and decay serve to nurture new life. Every one of Mother Earth's children co-operates so that the family survives.

I've paraphrased this oral teaching in many of my writings, each time gaining a deeper understanding of its meaning. So much is encoded, suggested and embedded in these words it's difficult to know where to begin when reflecting on it. I will never be sure I've extracted all the wisdom possible out of this passage. However, I will share what I've understood so far.

This excerpt shows us another way of understanding concepts of family and community. Family is more than our blood relatives; our community is broader than just our species of two-leggeds. As human beings we're connected to and interdependent on each other as well as on a huge complex web of life – on the Earth and beyond. No one exists as an individual; we all contribute to each other's wellbeing -- or ill health -- depending on what we think, say and do.

The teaching also emphasizes our roles and responsibilities to each other. Each member of the family or community has a role and a responsibility that serves the big picture and contributes to our collective survival. Responsibility in this sense is not a burden but something that actually enhances our life experience. The word literally means "ability to respond." In the relational framework we might understand responsibility as the ability to respond *appropriately* – that is, for the common good. In this sense, responsibility is seen as preferable to individualism, which doesn't really exist.

"Diversity," in the Indigenous mind, is not something to be simply tolerated. Nor is it something that merely benefits us in abstract or esoteric ways. Diversity in this paradigm is a matter of continued existence. We need our differences to survive, thrive and create. Difference is not seen as a point of tension but as essential to the functioning of the whole.

In my experience, the Indigenous definition of life is much broader than that of the dominant scientific paradigm. For us "life" is whatever is imbued with spirit (whatever vibrates with energy) and includes mountains, waters and the Earth Herself. We see entities, "beinghood", in what mainstream thinking might regard as lifeless objects. As Vine Deloria notes, "I think Indians [sic] experience and relate to a living universe, whereas Western people, especially science, reduce things to objects, whether they're living or not. If you see the world around you as made up of objects for you to manipulate and exploit, not only is it inevitable that you will destroy the world by attempting to control it, but perceiving the world as lifeless robs you of the richness, beauty and wisdom of participating in the larger pattern of life."[15]

Even in the material sense inter-dependence and interconnectedness are easy to understand. Environmental science makes our relationship to life on the planet very clear. We really don't control the environment but are part of it. What we do to the land, for example, eventually impacts our food chain, our water and air – even if it happens half a world away. Witness rising radiation levels on the west coast of North America caused by the Fukishima nuclear power plant accident. What we do to the environment today will impact generations to come. Your skin does not delineate the border between your body and the world around you. What the environment suffers comes home to roost in your body. You can't pour toxins into the air, irradiate the waters or otherwise impact the food chain without suffering the consequences. In relational worldviews, the environment is a part of us and what we do to "Our Relations" we do to ourselves. That concept is now well accepted in the dominant culture and can serve as a basis for beginning to understand the worldview of relationality.

Balance is also considered an important value in relational thinking.

---

[15] Jensen, Derrick. "Where the Buffalo Go: How Science Ignores the Living world: an Interview with Vine Deloria." Published in *The Sun*. July 2009. http://www.derrickjensen.org/work/published/essays-interviews/where-the-buffalo-go/

Since we are all affecting each other in a complex web of relationships, ensuring some sort of give and take (reciprocity) in our interactions with one another and the natural world ensures the common good. Hence, in my teachings I've been instructed in how to "put down" tobacco before gathering food or medicines from the bush as a way of reciprocating for those gifts. We "feast the dead" (share food with ancestors and each other) at various times throughout the year to give back to entities that we believe guide and help us from the spirit world. Ceremonies that take place before, during and after a hunt are partly about thanking the spirit of the fallen game and appreciating the sacrifice of life. The same is true of harvest and planting ceremonies. "Life feeds life, but spirit never dies," as the lyrics to one of my songs goes.

Sharing and generosity are hugely valued in Indigenous societies, as evidenced by practices such as the once outlawed potlatch, practiced by a variety of peoples on the West Coast of North America. The potlatch is a gathering where folks share food and gifts with each other. The hosts at these gatherings sometimes give away *all* of their material wealth, including their most prized possessions. The idea is that giving brings honour. Wealth is not about accumulating; it's about what one can give. To me hosting potlatch is a remarkable act of trust in the strength of one's relationships to community and a demonstration of faith in the principles of abundance and reciprocity.

Balance and reciprocity are considered in all our relationships including the one we have with ourselves. To be a healthy human being one must attend to the wellbeing of the body, mind, emotions and spirit, recognizing that when one of these aspects of self becomes unwell it throws the whole person out of balance. For example, feelings of depression have physical symptoms. The feeling of fear influences our decision-making. Physical pain impacts our emotions and we may get cranky, impatient or depressed. Indigenous healing practices are based in the recognition that all aspects of self comprise the whole human being.

Even though our wellness practices, involving dance, song and prayer were once ridiculed by the dominant medical establishment, holistic health care is increasingly seen as desirable and integrated approaches involving everything from music therapy to therapeutic touch to meditation are becoming more and more accepted as complimentary to conventional treatments in medical institutions. Generally, the holistic approach sees that mind, body and emotions interact and impact the wellbeing of the person. Holism also understands how physical and social environments, including those of the past, impact a person's wellbeing.

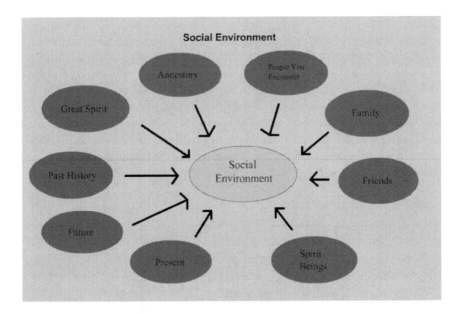

This relational way of understanding how the world functions, how life interacts, has implications for community sustainability. Looking to nature is an important survival strategy for Indigenous and other peoples. For example, in looking at Our Relations we emphasize how much cooperation (as opposed to competition) is necessary to sustain life.

Even some mainstream scientists are now questioning whether survival-of-the-fittest can actually be considered as a driver of human evolution. They note that there are many cooperative relationships in nature that enable both survival and "thrival." Surely, there are a gazillion examples of how animals within the same species cooperate to raise young, hunt, establish territorial boundaries and accomplish other tasks: Hyenas, dolphins, lions, wolves, whales, meerkats, elephants, bees … the list goes on. There are certainly endless instances of conscious and unconscious "teamwork" contributing to survival *and* evolution. Furthermore, in terms of awareness, there are studies such as those of zoologist Dr. Frans de Waal[16], which demonstrate that among primates, compassion and generosity are practiced, even when the creature doing the sharing does not itself benefit.

Cooperation across species is not as well known to scientists but they are beginning to study this phenomenon. In December of 2006 the

---

[16] Touber, Tjin, "Do Primates Feel Compassion?", Ode Magazine, Nov. 3, 2009. http://www.care2.com/greenliving/do-primates-feel-compassion.html as well as Sapolsky, Robert M., "Peace Among Primates", Fall 2007, Greater Good Science Centre – Article.
http://greatergood.berkeley.edu/article/item/peace_among_primates

science world was abuzz with the discovery that grouper fish and moray eels cooperate in hunts through signaling.[17] In one instance the eel consumes the prey whole while in another the grouper reaps the rewards of their joint effort. Biologist Bruce Lipton provides another example of cross-species cooperation when he discusses the relationship between a yellow shrimp that hunts while its partner gobi fish protects it from predators. Lipton also notes a species of anemone that rides atop the shell of a kind of hermit crab. The anemone shoots out poisonous darts to discourage potential predators and in return gets to eat the crab's leftovers.[18] The probiotic bacteria in your gut help you digest while they help themselves to your food.

The Three Sisters are how the Haundenosaunee (Iroquois) refer to a set of staple foods they've relied on for centuries: corn, beans and squash. To this day, these three seeds are planted in the same mound together as part of a sophisticated, sustainable practice that ensures long-term soil fertility and a balanced diet. Bean stems wind their way around cornstalks, stabilizing them, while enriching the soil with nitrogen. Squash vines remain close to the ground and shade emerging weeds, preventing their growth, while trapping moisture in the soil. Residue that remains from the harvesting of these three foods also enhances the soil conditions for future agricultural endeavors. This is one example of how the plant world cooperates and how their cooperation contributes to our wellbeing.

Yes, you will always find examples of competition in nature. One species will hunt another for food, for example. Yet if one considers the above teaching, "even death and decay serve to nurture new life," we see an overall framework where an animal's death is a form of cooperation enabling life to go on. A balance of life and death must be maintained to enable wellbeing. Hence the emphasis in Indigenous lifeways on taking only what is needed and using all of what an animal has to offer after a successful hunt.

Scientists are increasingly seeing Evolutionary Theory through these lenses. Dr. Daniel Grunbaum, an oceanographer at the University of Washington, believes that the role of violence in evolution has been overestimated. He notes that those nature documentaries showing animals fighting, hunting and killing each other only represent a small percentage of the creature's lifetime. Most of the time these animals are respectfully

---

[17] MacKenzie, Deborah. "Eels and groupers hung better together". New Scientist. December 2006. http://www.newscientist.com/article/dn10730-eels-and-groupers-hunt-better-together.html and "Fishy Cooperation: Scientsts Discover Coordinated Hunting between Groupers, Giant Moray Eels", Science Daily, Dec. 6, 2006. http://www.sciencedaily.com/releases/2006/12/061206095317.htm
[18] Lipton, Bruce H. *Biology of Belief: Unleashing the Power of Consciousness, Matter & Miracles.* Hay House, Ind. 2005. Page 13.

accommodating each other or cooperating.[19]

Indigenous peoples around the world took note of what they saw in nature and understood the significance of cooperation to the survival of life. In the Haundenosaunee Creation Story, Muskrat lost his life bringing mud up from the bottom of the ocean so that Sky Woman could survive on Turtle's Back. To many Indigenous peoples sacrifice to support life is highly valued and appreciated. It is also considered a form of cooperation.

Yet, I don't want to generalize about nor idealize Indigenous cultures, paradigms and values. Our nations had differences, conflicts and violence before the colonizers came along. Today, many First Nations communities rationalize operating casinos that contribute to their local economies by noting that competitive games of chance are part of the culture of many nations.

In reality, we have to admit that both cooperation and competition are intrinsic to "human nature" and human societies. We are clearly capable of both. The question is whether cooperation or competition contributes more to advances in human social, mental and physical development. The science that we will explore in upcoming chapters overwhelmingly suggests that cooperation is what drives human evolution, progress and wellbeing. That's a huge teaching that can be applied to how we organize activist communities and society generally.

In any case, you can see that how you understand the roles of competition and cooperation, and how you see them in relationship to each other and to you, have implications for how you act in the world. To illustrate, I was taught as a child in Catholic school that "man" holds dominion over the rest of Earth's creatures, over even the Earth Herself. Whether this is an accurate interpretation of Catholic teachings is not something I can comment on but I can say it was taught to me. Of course, Catholicism is not the only source of such ideas. Ayn Rand is quoted as saying, "Man's [sic] reward ... is that while animals survive by adjusting themselves to their background, man survives by adjusting his background to himself."[20]

In this worldview all of Our Relations were created to serve humankind. This paradigm suggests that, as two-leggeds, our relationship to other life forms is one of superiority. We have the power and God-given permission to enlist other life forms into service for our wellbeing. Consequently, we are entitled to hunt creatures to extinction if that serves our needs, namely profit and pleasure. We have God's blessing, if we need it or our own if we don't, to extract resources that supposedly make human

---

[19] Dixon, Alex. "Birds Do It. Bats Do It",
http://greatergood.berkeley.edu/article/item/birds_do_it_bats_do_it/
[20] http://www.sad-heart-break.com/by/ayn-rand/

lives easier and more pleasurable. We even have Divine or our own permission to reshape the nature of life at the genetic level and to control the evolution of our and other species, if we so desire. Only after we have exhausted crucial resources and poisoned our food chain do we, as a society, begin to question the logic of our actions and the beliefs that direct them.

On the other hand, relational paradigms not only provide definition and meaning to our life experiences but also promote wellbeing and balance for all of life, especially for us two-leggeds. It is not that other worldviews do not promote wellbeing; it is not that other paradigms deny relationality. There are many worldviews compatible with relational ones. Certainly seeing the glass as half full is not always, despite the adage, a sign of optimism any more than seeing the glass as half empty is exclusively about pessimism. Neither way of seeing is "wrong" per se. It's all about understanding which way of seeing makes the most sense in terms of the situation you're in and outcomes you want, keeping in mind that situations and desired outcomes can change and so can your way of seeing.

Lets look at that adage around the half full/half empty glass, where to identify the glass as half full is seen to be optimistic but to identify it as half empty is considered pessimistic. However if you've been lost in the desert for three days and you're really parched, a half full glass of water might be cause for pessimism because you know your body needs more. At the same time, if you're a mother trying to get some fluids into her hyperactive son and he finally settles down enough to drink, the half empty glass he leaves behind might be cause for celebration – the optimist view. So that same half-full/half-empty glass will be judged differently, depending on your relationship to it and what outcomes you desire. Whether we experience optimism or pessimism in any given situation depends on the story we tell ourselves.

How we treat the Earth and Our Relations, what we value in our relationships, likewise depends on the stories that contextualize our existence. So, if the outcomes we desire for ourselves and our communities, including those yet to be born, are about survival of the species and a high quality of living for all, which worldviews make the most sense? I would argue that understanding ourselves as inter-connected and inter-related in a vast, complex and delicate web of life is one paradigm that leads to these outcomes. But if you believe that we are individuals who don't need to take responsibility for others, who are entitled to pursue our personal goals without concerning ourselves with the "common good," then what outcomes are you likely to get?

To further explain the relationality paradigm, we, as individuals, can only know ourselves in relationship to others. I can only know myself as a mother in relation to my children, for example. I can only experience myself as loving if I have someone to love. I can only understand myself as a female heterosexual in the context of a world where other genders and sexual identities exist. If maleness didn't exist, there would be no need to differentiate or conceptualize myself as female. Male and female define each other. Mother and child define each other. Left and right define each other – even in the political arena.

Who are we without each other? How do we "create" each other? How have you constructed your identity, defined your purpose and articulated your goals in relation to others? How has your role as an activist been "created" by those whose values are contrary to your own?

In an episode of the *Babylon 5* science fiction TV series an interrogator puts one of the lead characters through a kind of trial to test her capacity to play the role she is destined for in the future. The trial begins with the question, "Who are you?" The Delenn character responds in turn with "I am Delenn." "I'm the ambassador from Minbar." "I'm the daughter of –." She is punished with an electric shock for all of all her responses, which are considered incorrect.[21]

One of the questions that occurred to me as I watched this scene for the first time was, how do you define who you are if you don't refer to your relationships? How do you answer the question "Who are you?" without referring to what people call you, your function in society or how you fit into a family, and so on?

How can I understand myself as giving if I have no one to gift? How do I understand myself as angry if there is nothing to be angry about? How do I understand myself as a social justice activist if I'm not taking action to create social justice for society?

I don't know what the writer of that Babylon 5 episode was thinking but from a relational point of view the "correct" answer to "Who are you?" might be, "I am you; I am she; I am we."

Being in relationship does more than lend definition to who we are. It enables us to experience spiritual growth as well as the joy of supporting the growth of others. For instance, just by being my children, my sons have allowed me to experience motherhood in all its height and depth and breadth. When I allowed myself to observe the world through their eager, trusting eyes, they reminded me of simple truths I'd forgotten. They have taught me how to love better. Through my relationship with them I have experienced the changing roles, responsibilities and joys of being a parent as they have transformed through birth, infancy, early childhood, adolescence, adulthood and so on. They were the first to enable me to enjoy the wonders of unconditional love.

These are just some of many experiences I have had as a result of

---

[21] Season 2, episode 21, "Comes the Inquisitor".

my relationships. In being a mother I have grown and learned and experienced life in a way that wouldn't have been possible without my kids. Of course not every mother experiences motherhood in the same way. Also, not being a parent doesn't imply anyone has less opportunity to extract joy or meaning from their relationships. Mothering my three sons is my particular story. It's one of many relationships that define me in this life.

In befriending, experiencing or hearing the stories of other people, I might get to know myself better; my likes and dislikes, emotional triggers, limitations, and so on. I might want to consider all of my relationships as representing the potential for a wonderful opportunity for adventure; the type of adventure that relating to computers, video games and i-phones could never provide. Through my relationships, I experience and offer opportunities for spiritual growth.

An excerpt from a Basis of Unity document for a group I currently work with states: "We are grateful that Creator/Great Spirit/God/dess (etc.) gave us all to each other so that we may help each other survive, thrive and grow our collective wisdoms."[22] This reflects a core understanding of relationality and spiritual growth.

If we consider the relationships of an individual to community we further understand that both define each other, depend on each other and impact each other in countless ways. The dominant worldview in North America acknowledges this but undervalues it, stressing instead a form of individualism that is not responsible to community. Hence, we can legitimately argue about whether wealthy individuals and corporations have any inherent responsibility toward the communities in which they function, much less the larger society, despite the fact that they use and too often abuse commonly "owned" resources and receive many kinds of infrastructural and social supports that all taxpayers subsidize. How many political leaders, corporate magnates or celebrities get into positions of power and/or acquire wealth without the hard work and contributions of many, many, many other people? Why does society assign more value to their "work" than to that of their employees or than to that of Our Relations (the environment) without whom we could not survive?

So how we frame our relationship to the world around us, to community, to the Earth and to each other has implications for how we structure our societies as well as how we understand our roles and responsibilities to each other. Indeed, it has implications for how we understand who and what we are. Relational paradigms not only acknowledge this but emphasize the role this worldview plays in individual

---

[22] From the "Statement of Principles" of the group Gathering Weavers based in Toronto.

and community wellbeing.

Identifying relationships to social and economic power are crucial in activist culture as it enables us to identify and act to rectify injustices. Locating yourself in relation to power becomes important in terms of understanding how you relate to yourself and others. Hence, I share some relevant parts of my story in the next chapter to enable you to see how we are related.

CHAPTER THREE: MY ADVENTURES IN THE JEDI ACADEMY OF LIFE

"Social location" is a fancy word used in academia and social science for the part of someone's personal story that illuminates power relationships. Declaring your social location helps people consider how your relationship to social power in your life has shaped your experiences, your opinions about those experiences and your expertise in analyzing, critiquing and advocating for social change.

Your social location tells people how you relate to others in society; what roles, responsibilities and authorities they may or may not have to you and you may or may not have to them. It has to do with race, gender, class, spiritual beliefs, physical ability, sexual orientation as well as communities, nations or states with which you're affiliated. Your story and how it is told influences how you think of yourself, how others see you, and the relationship between the two. It also has to do with the interrelationship between life choices you make and the cards you have been dealt.

As we saw in discussing relationality, our stories matter. Stories help us define who we are and what roles and responsibilities we have to each other. They help us assign meaning to our life experiences. They help us understand each others' commonalities and differences and give us the opportunity to grow and support each other's growth.

Since I am writing specifically for activists and social justice advocates, particularly Indigenous, racialized and other marginalized folks in the North American context, I feel a responsibility to share my story in this book.

Zainab's story

My mother likes to say I've been an activist since before I was born because she recounts tales of going to Civil Rights demonstrations in the US when she was pregnant with me. Hence, my social and family environment clearly steered me toward being a social justice activist.

I was born in New York City, to a White mother and a "Black Indian" father. Measuring Indigenous blood quantum on my father's side of the family has always been an inexact science. Measuring African blood quantum was never an issue since we have always grudgingly accepted the One-Drop Rule (one drop of African blood makes you African-American) imposed by the US context in which we lived.

Suffice it to say that both my father's parents were mixed race with African, Indigenous and European ancestry and it is unlikely that anyone from my great-grandparents on down knew the exact percentages of any of it. Being enslaved can do that to a family. My father's parents died when he was young so his paternal half-Cherokee grandmother raised him and his siblings in a small Black community outside of Staunton, Virginia. She was over100 years old when she passed on and I was six when I last saw her.

My great, great Cherokee grandmother had been enslaved since birth alongside Blacks, Indians and Black Indians on the Reynolds tobacco plantation and had experienced emancipation as a child. She was aware of her Cherokee heritage but not connected to any indigenous community, as was the case with most of the "Black Indians" in Staunton – and there were many. My great grandmother raised my dad as a Baptist, although various gems of what I now recognize as Indigenous wisdom permeated her parenting, whether from the African or Cherokee traditions, I couldn't say.

I, however, was raised in an urban environment at the height of both the Civil Rights and American Indian movements. I spent several summers at my great grandmother's home outside of Staunton, not the most isolated location, but rural enough for a city girl to gain some land-based teachings.

While I was raised to be aware and proud of my Indigenous heritage, it was never presented to me as my primary cultural identity. My parents encouraged me to embrace my multi-racial background; a task that would have left me friendless in a terribly segregated society then governed by Jim Crow laws and an official policy of genocide toward Indigenous peoples. Indeed, what I learned of Cherokee and other Indigenous peoples came first in books – liberal and sympathetic, yet written from a Eurocentric worldview.

In the meantime I lived an urban lifestyle in the segregated Black or Hispanic neighborhoods of New York City and Philadelphia. Most Black and Hispanic people I knew acknowledged Indigenous heritage, but it never formed the core of their cultural identities, clearly a testament to the effectiveness of the genocide project perpetrated in the Americas. In fact, when I was growing up, identifying as "Black Indian" was often seen as an attempt to claim some sort of light-skinned privilege. With the Black Power movement at its height, I identified simply as Black in my high school years. Though when it came up I never denied Indigenous ancestry and felt pride in it. However, I was never presented with an opportunity to embrace the culture, connect with an Indigenous community or develop a relationship with the land.

Today I really wonder how Indigenous I can claim to be given that I am clanless, my Indigenous family history – African and Cherokee -- has been lost in the colonization process and I do not have a familial relationship with any land. I've come to understand that this self-doubt is common to urban mixed-race Indigenous people whether mixed with white or African ancestry. It is a consequence of genocide.

While my father's ethnicity played a dominant role in my cultural identity, I was less than inspired by his role as my father. Though I now understand his life was terribly difficult, growing up in the Jim Crow south in a family and community fraught with violence. As a result of being taunted as the darkest skinned among his siblings, I imagine my dad had a real issue with self-hatred. My only memories of him are as a dysfunctional alcoholic sabotaging his life and the love of his family. My mother left him when I was eight and I didn't see him again until we accidentally bumped into each other on the boardwalk at Coney Island when I was 14.

I didn't like him. I was angry, resentful and hurt. I saw him on and off after that, was happy that he managed to "sober up" when I was in my late teens, but we were never close. I was 20 when I learned he'd died alone in a boarding house, his decomposing body found when someone reported a smell coming from his room. My feelings about my father changed at that time and I became very sad about his life, especially when I learned more about his dysfunctional family dynamics.

My mother also survived an abusive family. Her mother was Portuguese, possibly born in that country. My grandmother's background is a bit mysterious in that after her parents died she was sent to work at a neighbouring farm. She was only about seven or eight years old at the time and worked on that farm for an unknown number of years until her newly-married, just-turned-18 older sister obtained legal custody of her. By my mother's accounts, my grandmother's life was idyllic before that farm and not much was shared about the years she spent there. My grandmother, despite her own café-au-lait skin and curly black hair, not only identified as white but was a serious racist. My mother bitterly recalls being force-fed all manner of hateful notions about Jews, Native Americans and the African-descended. I suspect grandma had her own self-hatred thing going on and more than a few brown skeletons in her closet but I can't prove anything.

My mother's father was half Scottish and half Amish as well as a card-carrying member of the Ku Klux Klan. Shocking, I know. His Amish father had fled an abusive home at the tender age of 12, found work on a Scottish man's farm and married the farmer's daughter. By my mom's account, her grandfather managed to reproduce the domestic abuse he had fled.

Mom's childhood was fraught with violence and dysfunctionality too. Authorities came a few times to the door of her family home investigating my mom's broken collarbone and other injuries. Though she did not heap on me, my brothers and sister the full abuse she suffered, mom was not exactly the model disciplinarian. But what parent is? (Except for me, of course.) Yes, she used violence to discipline us, but unlike my mother's body, mine does not bear any permanent scarring.

Today I respect and appreciate what my mother did for us, working two jobs, sometimes making herself sick, to ensure we had food on the table. I find myself grateful for the strength she role-modeled. Needless to say her parents did not approve of her marriage to a Black-Indian and disinherited her. I met my grandparents only a couple of times when I was in my early teens and they were probably in their sixties. He was stoic and cold. She was fussy and controlling, encouraging my siblings and I to marry white so that we could lighten the family. They visited us so that their neighbours wouldn't see my mom dragging us brown children to their door. Meeting my grandparents made me appreciate my mother's spirit of survival.

Though raised in a Protestant tradition, my mother converted to send me to Catholic school because the academic standard was higher than in New York City's public schools. She also regarded Catholic schools as "safer," though I have never before or since experienced anti-Black racism from students, teachers and parents alike that was as vicious as what I experienced in the predominantly white Catholic school.

I was in the public system by the time I went to high school, being bussed from a Black community outside Philadelphia in an effort to integrate a formerly all white suburban school. I got beat up a lot. Let's just say it was a traumatizing yet character-building experience. It was in this phase of my life that I made a commitment to political activism, mostly to the Civil Rights/Black Power Movement. I attended protests, did strike support and fundraised for various causes. I can't say I ever particularly distinguished myself as a political activist in the sense that I took a leadership position or enjoyed any significant fame. In the beginning I was, of course, too inexperienced to take on leadership roles. Later, as I gained experience, I became too angry to sustain being any kind of role model, much less engender the necessary trust and respect that leadership requires.

The most memorable action of my teen years as an activist was when I co-organized the occupation of my high school's administration wing demanding more African American content in the curriculum and African Americans to teach it. That "sit in," as it was dubbed by local media, lasted about twelve hours before the cops came and "dispersed" us, arresting some and chasing away others.

These movements shaped my framework of analysis when it came to studying Indigenous history and culture in later years. My familiarity with the American Indian Movement (AIM) was a long distance one (fundraising and information sharing) and I cannot say that I thoroughly understood the fundamental struggle. Even if I did, I would have still been positioned as an outsider to it. I was generally supportive but in terms of concrete activism there was just nothing going on where I lived that provided me with the opportunity to become seriously involved in the parallel processes of developing a relational worldview as I engaged in activism. In university I was politically active in solidarity work with Central American struggles (a manifestation of Indigenous resistance to the genocide there) and the South African anti-Apartheid movement.

To protect my 16-year old brother (already a veteran of the local "Juvie Hall," a detention centre for youth) from being harassed and abused by Philadelphia's finest, my mother fled with him in the middle of the night to Montreal and later settled in Toronto. It was 1973. I was a teenager and had the choice of joining her but I was living with my boyfriend at the time and ... well, I was young and had different priorities.

I eventually did come to Toronto in 1975, six months pregnant with a total of $50 in my wallet. The half African American, half Puerto Rican baby daddy had just been arrested on charges I still believe were trumped up, having been caught in a drug raid while at a party and subsequently charged with dealing and resisting arrest. But Rico (as we'll call him) had given up using and dealing by the time we had hooked up. Eye witnesses to his arrest told me he was one of several young Black men who were dragged out of the party that night and beaten to a bloody pulp despite offering no resistance. He was only 19 at that time and he would not get out of prison until his 40's. Such is justice in the good old USA.

Our child was born with several congenital problems: micro-cephalic, visually impaired, with a cleft palate and hair lip. The possible causes bothered me for years and I puzzled at how it could have happened given that I was neither a drug user nor a drinker and the father had been clean and sober while we were together. Such questions are no longer an issue for me as my entire worldview has since shifted. In any case I knew I would never be able to go back home to the States because I'd never be able to afford my son's medical care. With my mom's support, (she was a citizen by then) I settled in Canada, which has universal health insurance.

In 1980s Toronto, I worked as a medical lab technologist to put myself through university part time. In six years I'd earned a B.A. in Latin American Studies without encountering a single student who identified as Indigenous or First Nations. There were no Aboriginal campus groups and I tended to identify and hang out with other racialized students. It was in this context that I was introduced to Marxism and developed an anti-racist, feminist, class analysis. This academic, Eurocentric framework shaped my early understanding of Indigenous struggles. I came to work within "The Left," though I was never entirely comfortable with it, but lacking a connection to anyone or anything Indigenous, I was unable to develop a critical analysis of something that just didn't "feel" right.

It wasn't until my mid-30s, after marrying a Canadian and giving birth to two more sons (healthy) that I put concerted effort into absorbing oral histories, songs and teachings of Elders. Thus, I was finally able to put a name to my worldview: "Indigenism." I have been active in Toronto's Indigenous community ever since. Initially I was resistant to identifying as a "Cherokee," despite pressure from many of my friends and colleagues to do so. I compromised by identifying as "Black Cherokee," which most people accept, even though there is no common understanding of the term. Today I prefer to identify as African American with Cherokee heritage.

The Indigenous community in Toronto, like most urban Aboriginal communities, is comprised of many alienated, traumatized and disconnected mixed-race people from a variety of backgrounds and experiences, all of which have left them struggling to come to terms with their cultural identities. It is a community in which I fit quite nicely.

My life shifted dramatically as a result of becoming involved in the Indigenous community. On the heels of the disintegration of my marriage I plunged myself into learning songs, stories and traditions of mostly Anishinaabe and Haundenosaunee peoples, since there was no Cherokee community in Toronto. Among my activities was to spend about a year as an Elder's Helper to the Native Liaison Officer at the now-closed, maximum security Kingston Penitentiary for women. I learned a lot in that role as the Elder worked with the Native Sisterhood providing teachings, leading ceremonies and generally offering whatever support she could to incarcerated women. While serving in that role I met some amazing Indigenous women who lived on both sides of the bars.

I also sang with Haundenosaunee water drum groups in Wahta First Nation and Toronto, learning stories, songs and dances as well as snippets of the language. In general, I attended ceremonies, teachings and gatherings absorbing wisdom from a variety of Elders, artists and wise people. I got to a point where I was asked by organizations to facilitate ceremonies and sharing circles for the community, which was a high honour for me. Looking back on it now, though, I'm stunned that I was able to pull off leading Full Moon Ceremonies at Anduhyaun Women's Shelter or sharing circles at Nekanaan Healing Lodge given how little cultural and spiritual knowledge I had at the time (and still have). Yet I managed to play a role in people's healing journeys and for that I will be forever grateful. Taking the lead in these ways also facilitated my spiritual growth. It was an acknowledgement of what I had always believed; that in helping others the helper grows, learns and transforms. An act of giving is an act of receiving and vice versa.

I still feel as though I have a lot to learn, a healthy mindset that motivates me to continue growing. In any case, I shifted slowly over time from a place of wanting to absorb information and get grounded in "the culture" to wanting to give back and share. I became an Indigenous sovereignty activist and while my definition of what sovereignty is shifted over time, I remained committed to supporting mostly land-based struggles such as the Six Nations land reclamation, the Ardoch Algonquin struggle against uranium mining exploration on their territory and later a national organization called Defenders of the Land[23]. While living in Toronto I worked with both Indigenous and non-Indigenous activists to raise awareness of issues, support people in struggle and protest actions taken by government, police forces and so on to raise awareness and stop the ongoing theft of Indigenous resources.

This work became so all-consuming that I fell seriously ill for eight months with a condition that was resolved through surgery. Despite spending a lot of time in excruciating pain, I now remember those months as magical in terms of my spiritual growth. I had been in constant motion for so many years, actively working, learning and doing that I had lost my ability to be still and present. Getting ill and then recovering required me to stay home and rest for almost a year. I experienced amazement at how much one can learn from just spending restful time alone in the quiet dark.

In my interactions with the healthcare system I came to understand how empathy, compassion and basic social skills are often lacking in our institutions. Plus, the fundamental approach of mainstream medicine seems inadequate and flawed.

First Nations, traditional Chinese and other alternative approaches to wellbeing have generally proven much more healing for my family and myself. These traditions are based in the mind/body connection. As I benefited from these healing approaches I further came to understand that taking personal responsibility for my health and working toward community wellbeing are inseparable.

Once I became well again, I upended my whole life, as in one of those fits of madness that characterize mid-life crisis stories. As my kids moved out on their own, I quit the job I wasn't happy with, applied for writing grants, took writing courses, focused on developing new and healthier relationships and descended into a level of soul-wrenching poverty and debt I'd never known before. At the same time I grew my knowledge, my skills and my wisdom. Alas, still in debt, I now know and like myself better than ever, which brings me a great sense of groundedness.

Today, though more experienced and, theoretically, wiser I struggle as much with identity, personal and political issues as I did when I was 15. My Indigenous worldview sometimes makes it difficult for me to interact as

---

[23] Website: http://www.defendersoftheland.org/

an intimate in urban Black communities. My lack of connection to a landed Indigenous community sometimes makes it difficult for me to find a complete sense of belonging in Indigenous circles. I constantly grapple with the implicit responsibilities of having Indigenous ancestry from both Turtle Island (North America) and Africa, as well as coming to an understanding of Indigenism through intellectual processes, oral teachings and occasional ceremony rather than lived experience on the land in community.

In general I see my journey as one of many Indigenous stories lived out within the context of colonialism and genocide. There are similar and not so similar stories out there but they are all part of the Indigenous experience on Turtle Island. I share the concerns of a variety of marginalized and vulnerable communities and am personally invested in seeing all of us become healthier. If there is one truth I have come to with age, it is that Indigenous paradigms have great potential to heal self, communities and the land.

It is with this hope of collective healing and transformation that I have written this book in order to share some remarkable information that, if taken seriously, has the potential to transform social justice work, our communities and the world.

CHAPTER FOUR: THE INTERNAL FORCE

One of the exercises I ask people to try when I'm leading workshops or speaking about my writings is something I've dubbed "Long Fingers." I adapted it from a podcast exercise featuring Qigong Master Chunyi Lin and there may be information online demonstrating his technique. My version goes like this:

1. Close your eyes and find the rhythm of your heartbeat.
2. To your heart's rhythm take in a breath for 4 beats.
3. Hold that breath for 6 heartbeats.
4. Exhale for 8 heartbeats.
5. Cycle through inhaling and exhaling (steps 2 through 4) a total of seven (7) times. You may notice your heart slowing down. That's both normal and desirable.
6. After your 7th exhale put your hands together in the prayer position, ensuring that you line up/match up the lines at the bottom of your palms. Most people will notice when they do this that the fingers of one hand tend to be a smidgen longer than those on the other. If your fingers are the same length there's no need for concern. It just means you're in a minority (and, being an activist, you should be used to that).
7. Make note of which hand has the longer fingers.
8. Decide you want to lengthen the shorter fingers.
   If your fingers are the same length pick a hand and decide you are going to lengthen the fingers of that hand.
9. Take your hands apart and shake them both, loosely – in any way that feels comfortable to you.
10. While you're shaking your hands repeat aloud "Long fingers, long fingers, long fingers …"
11. After about 15 seconds of this put your hands together again in prayer position as before, matching/lining up the lines at the bottom of your hands.

12. Note whether one set of fingers is still longer than the other. Or note if you have successfully lengthened the fingers of your chosen hand.

Most people who try this with me find that the length of their fingers has changed, sometimes the taller fingers have actually switched hands. (A short woman asked me if the technique would work on her legs.) For a minority of people in my workshops and groups, there is no change at all. Later we'll discuss some reasons why this exercise may not have worked, as it doesn't in some cases.

However, if you find a change in the length of your fingers (and I know this exercise hardly qualifies as controlled, empirical research but suspend that thought for a moment) think about what could possibly be the explanation for this. Would you be willing to concede that this might be an example of the capacity of the mind-body relationship?

Whatever your answer, consider the placebo effect, which is a phenomenon that has been known to modern medicine since 1955. Yet, as biologist Dr. Bruce H. Lipton notes in *Biology of Belief*, there has been very little research into why placebos generate the healing results that they do.

A placebo is an inactive substance or procedure used as a control in research experiments. The placebo effect occurs when health is improved by this "fake" treatment rather than a conventional medical one. Such improvements are measurable, observable or felt. For example, when a sugar pill, salt solution or fake surgery brings about the same or better result as the real drug or procedure, this is considered the placebo effect.

Below are some interesting accounts of controlled medical studies into the placebo effect.

In 2002, the Baylor School of Medicine divided arthritis sufferers into groups that received different treatments. Two groups received conventional surgeries for their arthritic knees. The third group received a fake surgery where the patients were sedated, as in a real procedure. Incisions were made, sounds and staff behavior simulated the real thing yet no action was taken on the knees. The incisions were then sewn up as per an actual surgery. Patients in all three groups underwent the exact same post-operative treatment. While those who had received actual surgeries improved as expected, it surprised researchers to learn that the group that had undergone the phony procedure also improved to the same degree as those that had received real surgeries. Patients in all three groups were caught on camera running, jumping and playing basketball for a TV news story on the study. [24]

Placebos have been particularly successful in treating depression. Psychiatrist Dr. Andrew F. Leuchter is Director of Adult Psychiatry and professor at the UCLA Neuropsychiatric Institute and Hospital. The American Psychological Association quotes him as saying "People have known for years that if you give placebos to patients with depression or other illnesses, many of them will get better." [25] He believes that a person's decision to seek treatment, their hope about the treatment, as well as positive interactions with health-care workers could all contribute to the placebo effect. In commenting on a study regarding the impact of placebos on depression Leucheter said, "What this study shows, for the first time, is that people who get better on placebo have a change in brain function, just as surely as people who get better on medication." [26]

Medical literature is full of stories about how placebos given to sufferers of all types of maladies are as effective as drug treatments. "It inevitably disturbs pharmaceutical manufacturers that in most of their clinical trials the placebos, the 'fake' drugs, prove to be as effective as their engineered chemical cocktails," says Dr. Lipton.[27]

Lipton also discusses the *nocebo* effect in his writings, which is the opposite of the placebo effect. That is, if people believe that what they are ingesting or what is being done to them is harmful, they will experience corresponding symptoms.

To illustrate he recounts a study where Japanese children allergic to a poison ivy-like plant had a harmless but similar-looking plant rubbed against their skin. They developed the same rash reaction they would have

---

[24] Lipton, Biology of belief, p.108-109.
[25] "Placebo alters brain function of people with depression", American Psychological Association, March 2002, vol. 33, no. 3, p. 16.
[26] Ibid.
[27] Lipton, Biology of Belief, p. 108.

had to the poisonous plant even though the actual plant they had been exposed to was harmless. Such is the power of belief on our bodies.

Medical case studies recounted in Lipton's works, as well as in many other books, journals and institutional websites, testify to the placebo effect. You may have your own placebo stories based on your experiences. The American Cancer Society reports that despite some skepticism still remaining in the health care sector, "there are studies showing that the placebo effect *is* real. For example, scientists have recorded brain activity in response to placebos."[28]

Pre-colonial Indigenous healing practices recognized the placebo effect, although it wasn't labeled as such. As noted above, the relational worldview does not separate mind from body from emotions – or spirit. So of course we believe that what you think and feel impacts your wellbeing – potentially either playing a role in causing illness or healing it. In describing her experiences with Indigenous healing modalities Sto:lo Elder educator and author Lee Maracle once said to me, "Our people know how to talk to the body." She explained that in her language it was impossible to tell someone they were sick or mentally ill. To describe a state of what we consider to be unwellness her people would say something like "you're out of rhythm with the Earth" or "you're not walking well on the land".

In terms of mind/body connection, we discussed earlier that in some Indigenous worldviews every individual is comprised of four inter-related components: mind, body, emotion and spirit. It is the quality of the relationships among the components of self, as well as the self's relationship to the social and physical environment, that determine wellbeing. In this sense, wellbeing is not a static state that one can achieve and live in forever. Wellbeing is about flux, shifts and adjustments to our ever-changing interactions. Our thoughts and emotions are always shifting and changing in response to each other, the environment, our bodies, etc. Our physical self is never static as there are ongoing activities of self-regulation and self-repair in a process called *homeostasis,* which is the body's tendency to maintain stability. Wellbeing is the ongoing shifting that comprises your responses to life. When you become unable to respond appropriately you can become unwell. Or you can become unwell when your environment (potentially including family and extended community) is unable to respond appropriately, making you unwell. Wellness is essentially about your relationships to yourself and the world around you.

What is sometimes remarkable to non-Indigenous folks is that in our understanding of wellness, a person can die "healed." As discussed earlier, death is a part of the natural cycle of Creation and if you resonate

---

[28]http://www.cancer.org/Treatment/TreatmentsandSideEffects/TreatmentTypes/placebo-effect

with natural rhythms and patterns you are considered well. Death is not the end of anything, it's a normal, natural and desirable transformation when viewed from the perspective of maintaining sustainability and ensuring the ongoing regeneration of life.

Modern medical practitioners increasingly understand that our thoughts and feelings play a significant role in wellness - as medical research demonstrates. Take stress as an example.

There are many studies and a fair bit of urban legend that make up our common knowledge about how thoughts and feelings related to stress impact our bodies. Anyone who has ever taken a stress workshop, read a book on the topic or downloaded online resources knows what happens to our bodies when we are stressed. We go into a fight/flight/freeze (FFF) reaction. Over the long term when we can't or don't manage our stress or stressors, our health suffers. Some ways we're affected include: many types of illness, accelerated aging, depressed immunity, inhibited ability to metabolize nutrients, inhibited ability to think clearly, irritability, weight loss or gain, memory loss, decreased libido, inhibited creative and problem solving capacity, compromised capacity to heal from tissue damage and so on.

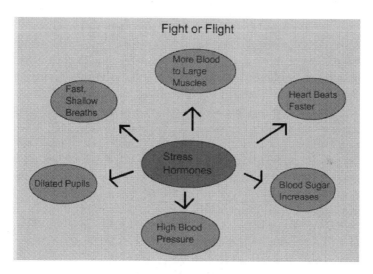

Stress is at the root of many conditions such as high blood pressure, insomnia, heart disease, depression, cancer and other health problems. Your heart pumps harder and more erratically when under stress. Like most people, you probably sense a quickened heartbeat and faster breathing when experiencing emotions like fear, anger, anxiety, worry, grief, shame, guilt, frustration, hatred and others. Bodies under stress experience a particular type of blood chemistry that includes high amounts of cortisol and adrenaline, which heighten your senses and improve the performance of your large muscle groups so you can respond to life threatening situations. However, cortisol and adrenaline can cause health concerns if they are present in your bloodstream at elevated levels for too long.

New information indicates that prolonged stress even biases the brain structure toward negativity, further jeopardizing mental, emotional and physical health. For example, if you are stressed out over a long period of time, parts of the brain that tell your body to secrete cortisol and adrenaline in response to your stressors will get bigger and more efficient while other parts of your brain that direct the biochemistry of calm, compassion and peace will shrink and not do their job as effectively. We'll look more in depth at this in the Chapter entitled "Jedi Brain Tricks."

In sum, long-term stress compromises your health and shortens your lifespan while inhibiting your mental capacities. We've known this for a long time, some cultures longer than others, but science is only beginning to understand the intensity with which thoughts and emotions can interact with our bodies. In fact, our thoughts and emotions can even interact with the bodies of others, which we'll look at in the "Intersecting Force Fields" chapter.

In *Spontaneous Evolution*, Lipton and Bhaerman cite case studies of people diagnosed with multiple personality disorder, officially known as Dissociative Identity Disorder (DID) where many personalities share one person's body. The psychiatric diagnosis of DID describes a condition in which a person displays multiple distinct identities or personalities, each with its own pattern of perceiving and interacting with the environment. The personalities are sometimes called "alter egos" or "alters".

This condition has been depicted in popular films like *Fight Club* where (spoiler alert) the antagonist is revealed to be the lead character's alternate personality. Norman Bates in *Psycho* suffers from DID as does Gollom in the *Lord of the Rings* trilogy.

As scanning and other scientific tools designed to observe what's going on in the brains of people diagnosed with DID have developed, some astounding information has been uncovered. For instance, normally each individual has a unique electroencephalogram (EEG/brain wave) profile. The EEG profile is understood to be as specific to a person as fingerprints. Yet in DID patients, we see several profiles within one body, as each personality generates its own set of brain waves. It is as though the body was a web navigator on your computer, a framework in which several tabs and windows open onto different websites, each containing completely distinct information arranged in completely distinct ways.

There are case studies in the medical literature where one personality of a DID patient has an allergy, including all the corroborating symptoms and blood chemistry. Yet other personalities in the same body do not have that allergy. Even more remarkable are the medical accounts of people with DID who have changed eye colour as they've switched personalities! Scars on the skin have come and gone with the shifting of personalities![29]

Thus, an increasing number of scientists have concluded that our thoughts and emotions impact not only our biochemistry and physical structure but our genes as well. These new discoveries have given rise to a science called Epigenetics, the study of what impacts our genes and how.

The idea that genetic changes take generations to show up is now being questioned, as it is increasingly understood that genes may be nothing more than hardware, while epigenes, which react quickly to our environment, determine the behavior of genes. This is likened to loading software on a computer. While the hardware has the capacity to support many applications, what your computer actually does (or doesn't do) depends on the software you load onto it. Epigenes, then, determine how our genes behave.

The factors influencing how your genes function are found in their environment. Your genes' environment includes a great many of the molecules in your bloodstream, some created as a result of your thoughts and feelings, conscious and unconscious. These molecules come and go in the fluids and cells of your body sometimes making physical alterations to your organs. These alterations may be momentary or long term. Your thoughts and feelings, physically manifested in the form of bio-electrical activity (a form of energy), impact your physical processes, determining what molecules appear in your body fluids. From an Indigenous framework, our thoughts and feelings arise out of our relationships.

You might ask, in light of epigenetic science, why can't we think our way into perfect health and immortality? Part of the answer to that question lies in the relationship we have to our conscious and subconscious thoughts, which will be explored in more detail later. Another part of the answer is that our thoughts and feelings are only two of many influences on our wellbeing and longevity.

For now, let's consider the idea of illness occurring, in part, because our relationships are unhealthy. These include our relationship with the components of self (mind, body, emotion and spirit) as well as family, community, ancestors, generations to come, other life forms in nature and a whole host of spirit beings. It may also be we get sick due to unhealthy relationships among communities.

This is not to say that we are to blame for our illnesses. Our relational networks are complex. For example, in the short film *Thirst*, Metis

---

[29] Lipton Ph.D., Bruce H. and Bhaerman, Steve. *Spontaneous Evolution: Our Positive Future (and a Way to Get There from Here)*. Hay House. 2009.

filmmaker Gail Maurice describes arriving at the northern Oji-Cree First Nation of Keewaywin, poised to lead a filmmaking workshop with youth. She notices that most of the children in the community have sores on their skin. Suspecting the cause might be in the community's drinking water, Gail collects some and has it tested. She finds the water that the community drinks, showers in and washes dishes with contains uranium.

Illnesses that result from drinking uranium-contaminated water in Keewaywin, are certainly not in any way the fault of the individuals who are sick. Instead the illnesses originate in colonial relationships that mainstream society has with land, resources and First Nations peoples. The relationship of colonial society to the Earth is one in which people are believed to have dominion over resources that exist to serve human needs and/or desires. This belief makes it less likely that resources are used sustainably and respectfully, as evidenced by the environmental issues our world is currently confronting. Furthermore, in this worldview, Indigenous societies are regarded as primitive and Indigenous lives as less valuable. The dominant society does not respect the inherent right of Indigenous peoples to live on their lands in healthy, sustainable ways. Furthermore, this way of thinking does not see that the lives of the people of Keewaywin are entangled with others on Turtle Island. Instead, they are treated as obstacles to progress and the accumulation of wealth. Consequently, we see an example of the ongoing genocide of the world's Indigenous peoples.

In the Keewaywin story we can see how we all collectively play a role in each other's wellbeing or illness. This is one way in which Indigenous paradigms differ from some of what passes for New Age "wisdom". Celebrity New Agers and self-appointed gurus have been known to fault the victims of tsunamis, earthquakes and hurricanes for their own suffering. Some stars of the movement have publicly stated their belief that the victims of "natural" disasters collectively engaged in thinking that brought disaster to them. The Indigenous teachers I've had in my life would strongly disagree. Many individuals, organizations and institutions have played a role in the situation First Nations communities now face, and collectively they share responsibility. In fact, we all share responsibility.

I'm sure I don't have to solidify my case further for social justice activists. I simply want to point out that there are significant differences between New Age philosophy and Indigenous wisdom. Even though many New Agers like to collect Indigenous teachings, repackage and sell them, in a form of spiritual colonialism, they have clearly misinterpreted some important tenets. Some of these tenets relate to the role of the heart within the body as well as in interpersonal relationships. In the next chapter let's explore how the heart's intelligence relates to the mind/body connection.

CHAPTER FIVE: JEDI HEART TRICKS

When I studied medical technology back in the late 1970's I was told that the brain was pretty much the body's control centre. All body parts communicated with the brain and the brain directed what went on in the organs and systems. The truth is, if you were to map out how communication operates in the body you'd end up with something that looked more like a three-dimensional spider web. Cells and organs communicate with each other as well as the brain in numerous ways including through bio-chemicals that circulate in our bloodstream and electrical impulses that are carried by the nervous system. The heart also receives messages from and delivers messages to all parts of the body and, as it turns out, is very much a centre of communication. In fact, more messages are sent from the heart to the brain then the other way around. Those messages are often directives to the brain, which then messages other parts of the body to respond appropriately to the situation. Thus, the heart plays a huge role in directing and coordinating activities in the body. At least that's one point of view.

Some scientists such as David Perlmutter, M.D. FACN actually reject the idea that either the heart or the brain play a central role in communication within the body. Perlmutter believes that there is more equity within the body's communication network than previously thought, citing that there are neurons (brain cells) in the lining of the stomach and that more neuro-transmitters are produced in the stomach and the liver than in the brain. His book *Power Up Your Brain* (co-written with medical anthropologist and shaman Dr. Alberto Villodo) emphasizes the role that diet, exercise and other behaviours have on the mind/body connection.

In any case, there are many levels on which your heart communicates with you body but your heartbeat is important in terms of what the heart has to say, especially to the brain.

HRV Coherence

The Institute of HeartMath further enlightens us on the mind-body relationship inherent to Indigenous and other relational paradigms. This nonprofit institute, based in Boulder Creek, California, is engaged in research and education around the mind/body connection. On their website you will see accredited scientists sharing peer-reviewed research on matters of the heart.

Researchers at the institute have been studying something called Heart Rate Variability (HRV), which is about measuring the uniformity and consistency of the interval between heartbeats and what impact it has on our bodies. What they have found is a remarkable relationship between emotions, heart rate and brain activity that have implications for wellbeing.

What we now know is that smooth and even heart rhythms make it easier for us to think better and make decisions. Encoded in every heartbeat is information about our emotional responses to our environment or perceived environment. Electrical signals from the heart inform the brain of what is going on all over your body. This is the process of an emotional reaction. It used to be thought that emotions were formed in the brain but new findings indicate that feelings result from the interaction between your heart and brain. (That's probably not the end of the story, as ongoing research will surely tell us.)

In any case the findings around what happens to HRV when you're under stress and in the fight/flight/freeze (FFF) response aren't surprising. The heart rhythm patterns of people in this state are irregular, chaotic or "incoherent." This incoherent heart rate signals the brain to ensure your body secretes cortisol and adrenaline, ramps up respiration and, sends extra blood to your large muscle groups and sensory organs at the expense of the higher thinking centres.

This is exactly what you want when you are in a dangerous situation and may have to run to stay safe or defend yourself from danger but you don't want to live your life under such conditions. Nor do you want to be triggered into this state when you don't need to be.

What researchers at the Institute of HeartMath have found is that a mere five minutes in the FFF state buys you six hours of depressed immunity, high blood pressure and the biochemistry of stress (such as high cortisol and adrenaline levels). It's certainly not the healthiest state to be in over the long term. If you are angry or depressed or otherwise stressed out on a regular basis, your health suffers.

What's also important to know about FFF is that your body can switch to this state in an instant, triggered by threats to your wellbeing - actual, perceived or imagined - as well as *memories* of threats to your wellbeing. For example, recalling dangerous, humiliating or frightening times in your childhood can result in this incoherent HRV state and all of its affects on your body.

Memories with strong emotional resonance can cause you to react to things that happened in the past rather than what is happening now. Hearing someone use the N-word, "Redskin" or "faggot," even on

YouTube, can enrage you when you associate that with memories of being taunted, humiliated or hurt by hateful people in your past. Even if you are not in a life-threatening situation at the moment, the perceived potential or future threat to you and your loved ones can slam you right into FFF mode.

Your brain remembers strong emotions and the situations in which they occur. So a mere smell, sound or taste associated with a strong feeling may trigger that same emotional response you had years ago and leave you terrorized, enraged or grief-stricken even when there is no real reason to feel that way. For instance, a whiff of perfume that reminds you of your math teacher might take you back to your high school years when the class laughed at you for getting the wrong answer. Feelings of humiliation and shame might re-surface and influence your decision about what to study at university.

Likewise, even imagining or fantasizing that you are in a situation that generates strong emotions like anger, fear, hate, grief, depression, etc. also generates the stress response. If you find a lump in your breast and start to imagine it is cancer, your body will react to the fear, frustration and anxiety your imagination generates. Actors have even been shown to undergo physical changes that correspond with the emotions they are *pretending* to have while playing characters in a fictionalized story. An actor who must show grief for the sake of the story may find her/his biochemistry reflects an actual state of grief.

HeartMath research shows the following consequences of what might be called "negative emotions" (although such emotions have their functions) such as less capacity to think clearly, less efficiency in decision-making, less ability to communicate clearly, reduced physical coordination, higher risk of disease, increased risk of high blood pressure and so on.[30]

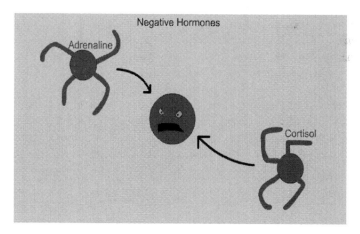

---

[30] ibid.

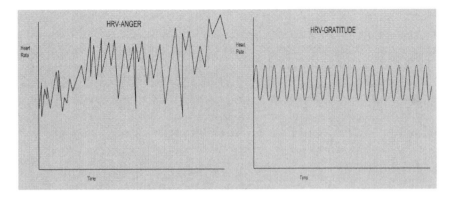

The opposite of incoherence is, of course, coherence. The figure above is an artist's representation of the heart rate variability of someone experiencing anger verses someone who is feeling thankful. The pattern on the left is described as incoherent or chaotic while the pattern on the right is considered coherent. Other HRV patterns of people in various emotional states are depicted on the HeartMath website.

According to HeartMath, "HRV Coherence" is the optimum state to cultivate and is significantly better for you than mere relaxation. When research participants are in this state their HRV scans show a smooth, consistent heart rate that corresponds with the best states of health. HRV coherence is an indicator of longevity and physical wellbeing. It can also be measured medically through biochemistry and brain imaging. In this state, you activate the involuntary (parasympathetic) nervous system, which generally slows or relaxes bodily functions.

What puts you into HRV Coherence? Many experiences including calling up fantasies, memories or thoughts that elicit feelings of generosity, gratitude, appreciation, love, forgiveness and other "positive" emotions.

While in HRV coherence (the opposite of being stressed out), calming molecules flood the bloodstream. Let's take a look at three of these: DHEA, oxytocin and nitrous oxide

DHEA

DHEA stands for dehydroepiandrosterone, the base hormone produced by the adrenal glands, essential to the production of steroids such as testosterone and estrogen. It is credited with functions such as slowing or reversing the aging process, enhancing athletic performance, preventing Alzheimer's disease, improving libido, fighting fatigue and enhancing health in people with HIV/AIDS. It has also been known to relieve unpleasant menstrual symptoms, address erectile dysfunction, stay osteoporosis and stimulate the immune system. In addition, DHEA plays a role in regulating blood cortisol levels, thus countering the stress reaction while promoting fat loss and muscle development.

It's relatively easy to learn about the impact that DHEA has on your health. The drug is manufactured and can be taken in pill form. However, invoking certain thoughts and feelings provides us with a naturally produced version, where we don't have to worry about side effects or overdosing.

Oxytocin

Oxytocin has been called the "hormone of love", the "bonding molecule" and the "cuddle hormone" as it influences our ability to bond with others. Dr. Dacher Keltner's research, from the University of California, indicates that oxytocin levels predict attachment behaviors; the higher the level, the stronger the attachment. The hormone is associated with both labour and breast-feeding, promoting mother-child bonding, but also plays a role in both men's and women's abilities to foster a sense of interpersonal connection.

The inhibited ability or inability to secrete oxytocin has been linked to psychological conditions characterized by a lack of capacity to care for others, empathize and feel compassion.

Any number of social interactions, mental states and emotions can trigger the release of oxytocin, promoting feelings of calm, trust and openness. The biochemical has a very short lifespan but can release again and again in response to what we're feeling, thinking or experiencing. Being with, or even thinking about being with, people we care for is enough to trigger the release of oxytocin.

When released by the heart or the brain, oxytocin lowers blood pressure and cortisol levels, helps us counter the stress reaction, decreases fear and even accelerates the healing of physical wounds.[31] In a 2005 study at the University of Wisconsin groups of women were given mild, but still painful, electrical shocks on their ankles. Women who were alone experienced anxiety before, during and after the shocks. While holding the hand of a stranger, women experienced a reduction in anxiety around the shocks. But women who held the hands of their partners ("husbands" in the study's language) while being shocked did not experience any anxiety and remained calm throughout the procedure.[32] Apparently the comfort and security women felt while in contact with someone they believed loved them actually decreased or eliminated their discomfort at being shocked.

Scientists are still trying to understand the differences in how men and women respond to and make oxytocin but it is clearly involved in social and

---

[31] Grahm, Linda. "Oxytocin: Helping the Brain Generate Feelings of Deep Connection and well-Being", Wise Brain Bulletin. 2008.
[32] Ibid.

sexual behaviours. Hugging, touching and sexual arousal raise oxytocin in both sexes. Apparently, kissing leads to rises in oxytocin for men but not necessarily for women. In one study where couples kissed for 15 minutes, cortisol in all participants decreased and oxytocin in men increased. Oxytocin levels in women, however, actually went down. Researchers speculated this was because the women's oxytocin levels were already high at the start of the kissing exercise.[33] Dr. John Gray suggests that males must balance oxytocin levels with testosterone in order to enjoy healthy inter-personal relationships. According to his research, women are found to be much more grounded and emotionally stable with higher levels of oxytocin than men with those same levels.[34]

Either way, the hormone is important to both sexes, although we need to be careful about generalizing as some scientists have done. Large quantities of oxytocin are found to be present in women who are involved in abusive relationships. Animals facing predators secret vast amounts of oxytocin and it is believed that this helps them prepare emotionally and physically for death, signaling a kind of surrender. There is speculation that oxytocin may have several roles to play in our bodies including decreasing fear in situations where fear might be an appropriate response.

In any case, it's clear that, assuming you are safe, the oxytocin produced when you are feeling connected, loved and cared for is very good for your health. Not only that, it promotes feelings of connection, trust and general wellbeing. It's furthermore essential to mother/child bonding.

Nitrous Oxide

Dr. Christiane Northrup, author, obstetrician and expert on women's health, calls nitrous oxide the "feel good" molecule. It has different but crucial roles in both the male and female orgasm. The more nitrous oxide you have in your bloodstream, the healthier you are and the better you feel. The better you feel the more nitrous oxide your body produces in an upward spiraling effect, without any apparent limits so long as the chemical is produced by our bodies. Nitrous oxide has a further role in connecting your conscious mind to your subconscious mind, resulting in higher levels of self-awareness and mind-body connectivity.[35] The placebo effect is believed to be partly reliant on high blood levels of nitrous oxide, which also increases the neuro-transmitters beta-endorphin and prolactin, both of

---

[33] Hight, Holly. "Kissing is Good for the Species", Cosmos Magazine. February 15, 2009. http://www.cosmosmagazine.com/news/2553/kissing-good-species

[34] Gray, John, Ph.D. *Mars and Venus on a Date*. Harper Paperbacks. 2005.
[35] Northrup, Christiane, MD. The Secret Pleasures of Menopause. Hay House. 2008.

which enhance positive moods. In addition, prolactin lowers blood pressure and promotes feelings of calm.

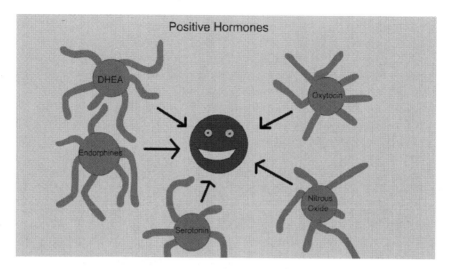

Mind/Body/Emotion Connection

Medical scientist, psychologist and expert in stress health, Dr. Joan Borysenko notes that the placebo effect is more likely to impact people who feel connected, loved and cared for[36]. The better you feel, the stronger the mind/body connection. The stronger your mind/body connection, the better you feel.

In the Long Fingers exercise at the beginning of this chapter, the breathing pattern we started with was designed to make you feel calm and relaxed, to encourage your body to produce these "feel good" molecules and increase your chance of lengthening your fingers. If you weren't successful at lengthening your fingers it might be an indicator you were in a temporary state of stress – or feeling cynical.

In any case, HRV Coherence is an indicator of the healthiest physical state of being. It is triggered by "positive" or pleasant emotional states such as gratitude, appreciation, and generosity. Even compassion, defined as caring concern and a desire to end suffering (not to be confused with pity or a stress-inducing concern), generates a state of coherence. This is what was going on with Matthieu Ricard when he meditated on compassion as recounted in the Preface. All you have to do to benefit from the biochemistry of optimum health is think, remember or imagine something

---

[36] "Wisdom of the Heart". An audio lecture posted on the website of the Institute of Noetic Sciences. June 7, 2005. http://www.noetic.org/library/audio-lectures/joan-borysenko-wisdom-heart-intimacy-love-and-1/

that calls up pleasant feelings. Even compassion generates a healthy biological response.

As mentioned in the Preface, HeartMath has found that five minutes of HRV coherence buys you up to five hours of enhanced immunity, healthful biochemistry and optimum healing. So five minutes of focusing your thoughts in a way that generates feelings of compassion, gratitude, appreciation and generosity promotes wellbeing. This would be true so long as you're not stressing yourself out to cultivate such feelings as in folks who are repressing or denying unpleasantness in their lives. Repression or denial of feelings generates a stress response. We will discuss how to deal with such emotions, which as we noted are sometimes healthy responses to our environment, in later chapters.

Other studies on the advantages of cultivating feelings of gratitude also conclude that there are psychological and physiological benefits such as greater alertness, focus and concentration as well as the capacity to exercise more and sleep better.[37] Dr. Jamil Zaki, a professor of psychology at Stanford University, has learned that giving someone chocolate and eating chocolate look exactly the same in your brain[38] (assuming you like chocolate).

Robert A. Emmons' research shows that grateful people are more stress-resilient, that is, less likely to stay in stressful states for long and able to recover from stress faster. Gratitude strengthens a sense of self-worth, according to Emmons, who makes a distinction between *feeling* grateful and *being* grateful.

Feeling grateful is a response to something pleasant that happens to you, as in the emotion you experience when you are given a gift or get a raise. Feeling grateful depends on something external to yourself, at least partially out of your control. You were offered the job, it remained sunny for your trip to the pow wow or it rained enough so your flower garden blossomed. The implication is that if you don't get the job or the sunshine or the rain when you want it, your mood might sour. In this sense feeling grateful is dependent on something pleasant happening.

Being grateful doesn't require anything to happen in order for you to feel thankful. A state of gratitude involves noticing and feeling blessed or appreciative for life and the small stuff, even when things aren't going your way. One can appreciate a new day of life, the roof over their heads as well

---

[37] R.A. Emmons & M.E. McCullough, *Journal of Personality and Social Psychology*, 2003, *84*, 377-389.

[38] Simon-Thomas, Emiliana R. "Three Insights From the Cutting Edge." Good Science Centre website. September 7, 2012. http://greatergood.berkeley.edu/article/item/three_insights_from_the_cutting_ed ge_of_compassion_research

as the sacrifices of life, time and labour represented in their daily meals. Being grateful doesn't depend on anything external happening. It's a state of being where you take the time, consciously notice and give thanks for the goodness or even attempted goodness in your life.

Ironically, this point becomes clearer when we think about the difference between *being* angry and *feeling* angry. Feeling angry implies we are in a temporary state, responding to something that didn't originate within us. You can feel a passing moment of anger when the kids track mud on the just-mopped floor, for instance. Seeing that someone has scrawled a hate message on the wall of your bathroom stall can elicit feelings of anger. *Being* angry is about experiencing a constant state of anger, which underlies your thoughts, words and deeds. This state of anger doesn't depend on external occurrences. It's an out-of-control, off balance way of being that limits your sense of joy and fulfillment. You may not necessarily notice that anger is your usual temperament. Even if you do, you may not be aware of the underlying cause. *Being* angry is a very unbalanced, ungrounded place to live.

Sometimes when I discuss anger and its effects with activists I get very defensive reactions. "I can be angry at the cops and then go home and have fun with my partner." "I can hate the rich and love the poor at the same time." "I love my people but I am so outraged by their stupidity."

When my boys were young their father and I used to read from a book that encouraged children to understand that they could feel two emotions at the same time, such as love and anger. That isn't, technically speaking, true.

Love and anger are two very distinct physiological states with completely different biochemistries, heart rhythms and brain activities. In *Biology of Belief* Lipton explains that at a cellular level we cannot experience a stress reaction at the same time that we are feeling generous or kind or compassionate. However, we can enjoy an underlying sense of appreciation for life while feeling temporary anger, frustration, grief and so on. You can *be* thankful that your life intersected with a loved one who has passed on and still *feel* grief and sadness about their passing, for instance. You can feel momentary anger at your partner for not doing her/his share of the housework and still care deeply about that person's overall wellbeing. But loving and hating at the same time? Not possible.

While it's good to cultivate a state of appreciation, what about people who seemingly have nothing for which to be appreciative? There are times and circumstances that challenge us all. This issue will be discussed more thoroughly in the "Shape-Shifting Tricksters" chapter but for now, let's just understand that I am not advocating anyone repress or deny their unpleasant feelings. Nor do I want to see anyone rush themselves through uncomfortable states of grief, sadness or fear in the interest of feeling good. We need to fully experience all of our emotions to enjoy wellness and safety. The issue for me is about claiming a general sense of optimism and openness about life. A sense of confidence that, even though we'd rather unpleasant things didn't happen, we will get through them and possibly emerge with greater capacity to weather future storms. We certainly shouldn't pressure ourselves to find silver linings in storm clouds. There are times when the healthiest response to a situation is to allow yourself to feel whatever comes up.

At the same time, as Helen Keller noted, "No pessimist ever discovered the secret of the stars or sailed an uncharted land or opened a new doorway for the human spirit."[39] Personally, I've been astounded by people who have survived or are surviving tremendously difficult life experiences who still find something for which to be thankful. It may only be that they're still alive, but they nevertheless feel that gratitude. I felt moments of it during my illness when I was in great pain and didn't know if I would survive. I felt grateful for the fact that my sons were taking responsibilities for the household. I appreciated friends who were supporting me. I felt thankful that my illness was pulling family members together.

By sharing this, I don't mean to compare my circumstances to anyone else's. There are many people in difficult situations who don't feel grateful and, of course, they're entitled to feel that way. I have no expectation that anyone confronting a significant challenge should feel thankful. Certainly not in the moment. I only wish to share that my own illness was made that much more bearable because I had the capacity to appreciate many things that were happening during that time and now that I am out of that incredibly painful moment I can appreciate the gifts I now find in the experience. After all, I'm sure that if I hadn't been sick that year I wouldn't have written this book.

Making a concerted effort to appreciate arriving alive to your daily destination, valuing your functioning senses or treasuring the presence of someone you see every day -- feeling thankful *just because*, this is *being* grateful. And it makes a difference to your physical health as well as to your mental and emotional state.

The literature on happiness sometimes discusses the concept of a "set point" which is a baseline happiness level to which you will eventually return after experiencing emotional highs and lows. Studies indicate that people who win big at lotteries, or become seriously ill or otherwise encounter a powerful emotional event will only temporarily experience a major shift in their overall emotional state. They will not undergo a permanent change to their basic temperament.

Definitions of happiness vary as do ideas on how set points get established or changed but in general the research suggests that if your set

---

[39] http://www.quotationspage.com/quote/32595.html

point is one of "being thankful" or if you can establish a state of appreciation as your baseline you're more likely to experience an overall sense of calm, hope and optimism about life – even in difficult circumstances. This backdrop of temperament allows you more emotional resiliency. You bounce back from stressful situations more quickly and are less likely to be bothered by minor stressors.

As an activist, you might ask if it's possible, ethical or desirable to maintain a sense of gratitude, peace and optimism in the midst of suffering. After all, it seems a bit callous and insensitive to cultivate inner peace when people around the world and at home are being impoverished, bombed or tortured. Does gratitude take away one's motivation to struggle for social justice?

Emmon's work shows it's possible to be thankful in the midst of suffering. Remember that compassion, defined as the desire to alleviate suffering in others, is an emotion that can generate an overall sense of peace. You can still be concerned about the pain of others and struggle for social justice while you maintain a general sense of appreciation for life and all its gifts. In fact, I struggle for social justice precisely *because* I appreciate, honour and respect what life has to give to us all. Life is even sweeter when we share its gifts with each other from places of empowerment rather than guilt, shame, fear, desperation, hatred or anger. My fundamental optimism and positivity about life are not separate from my desire to see others benefit from its blessings. Rather these feelings and desires are infused into each other. That's why I'm an activist. When I connect to my gratitude, I become a better activist.

Managing your feelings about suffering involves trusting yourself; trusting that even when others behave badly you won't be knocked too far from your centre. It involves trusting that you are grounded and will always return, as soon as possible, to a place of appreciation, compassion and generosity no matter what. It certainly doesn't suggest you become complacent with suffering – yours or anyone's. The moments of gratitude I experienced when I was ill did not dampen my desire to become well again nor did it deter me from pursuing all avenues to restore my health. The increasing sense of peace I now enjoy in my life does not dissuade me from working toward social justice.

Buddhist teacher and activist Thich Nhat Hanh has written: "To suffer is not enough. We must also be in touch with the wonders of life."[40] Indeed, I've marveled at how many who have survived the physical, mental and emotional traumas of Indian Residential Schools (boarding schools in the U.S.A.) make time every day to give thanks for the rising sun of a new

---

[40] http://www.redrat.net/thoughts/wtc/suffering.htm and http://www.cit-sakti.com/peace/peace-being-peace.htm

day, the waters that they drink or the continued presence of children in the family. I used to wonder how they could be so grateful for life when it had dealt them such a raw deal. Now I better understand.

First Nations ceremonies are all about thanksgiving. All ceremonies and traditional activities incorporate prayers of gratitude and celebration for the gifts we enjoy in life because focusing on these lifts the spirit and enables us to feel and think in ways that promote wellness. Somehow First Nations peoples knew this before any colonizers arrived in our lands. These ceremonies heal hearts, bodies and minds.

In my experience I've found that many activists aren't entirely comfortable with the adage that world peace establishes itself one person at a time. I'm not entirely comfortable with it either. Striving for social justice and world peace is by definition a collective project. Not to mention that my individual sense of peace is inseparable from that of My Relations, including my two-legged siblings. The slogan of the South African Congress of Trade Unions, outlawed by the apartheid state of South Africa in the 1960's, was: *An Injury to One is an Injury to All*. I'd bet this sentiment is grounded in an African Indigenous mindset and it is as true today as it was then. In any case, my understanding of working for world peace is about personal *and* social change. This is another feature that distinguishes the Indigenous teachings I've received from some New Ageism.

Does gratitude or any other positive emotion encourage passivity or complacency with one's condition in life? Emmon says no. He maintains that gratitude facilitates achievement. In one of his published studies participants identified six personal goals they intended to pursue in the next two months. These goals were related to academic attainments, personal relationships and health. Those participants assessed to be in a state of gratitude were 20% more likely to achieve their goals.

These and similar studies might contain some lessons for social justice activists. Might there be a relationship between the optimism and appreciation that activists personally embody and the success of social movements?

Similarly, the neuroscience of compassion, an emotion that also produces HRV coherence, is generating new and amazing discoveries that bear closer examination. Dr. Dacher Keltner, co-Director of the Greater Good Science Centre, defines compassion simply as the "concern to enhance the welfare of another who suffers or is in need." He differentiates this from empathy (a mirroring or understanding of other's emotions) and pity (a feeling of concern for someone felt to be inferior to oneself).[41]

---

[41] Keltner, Dacher. "Compassion, Mindfulness and Wellbeing." Powerpoint presentation. 2009.

Keltner maintains that compassion gets a bad rap in Euro- and North American-centric thinking. As noted earlier, we live in a competitive society that enshrines the evolutionary notion of survival-of-the-fittest. Yet Keltner believes that there was a second, less well-known theme that ran through Darwin's work, which might better clarify our understanding of the competitive nature of natural selection. The term *survival-of-the-fittest*, though mentioned in Darwin's writings, was a term actually coined by Herbert Spencer and other Social Darwinists. In this context, the concept was used to argue for the inherency of white supremacy. Keltner believes *"survival of the kindest"* better captures Darwin's thinking.

Whether Darwin's writings have taken on a significance he did not intend is arguable, particularly given that the original title of his 1859 publication was *On the Origin of Species by Means of Natural Selection, or the Preservation of Favoured Races in the Struggle for Life*. In any case, it's clear that evolutionary theory has often been used to counter calls for more compassion and generosity in our societies. There have been too many scientists who use evolutionary theory to justify racial, gender and other forms of inequality.

As discussed earlier, some schools of thought see compassion and generosity as barriers to progress and achievement. German philosopher Immanuel Kant, seen as a major contributor to the Enlightenment that influenced the Colonial (Founding) Fathers of the United States, saw compassion as a weak and misguided sentiment: "Such benevolence is called soft-heartedness and should not occur at all among human beings."[42] Libertarian author Ayn Rand, a celebrated hero to Tea Partiers and conservatives in the US said, "If any civilization is to survive, it is the morality of altruism that men [sic] have to reject."[43]

In any case, Keltner's work on compassion has significant implications for social justice. He has shown that compassion activates the vagus nerve, part of the parasympathetic (involuntary) nervous system. Stimulating what is called a *vagal response* slows the heart rate and generates feelings of inter-connectedness, bonding and basically puts one into what HeartMath calls an HRV coherence state. This centred, focused, peaceful state provides an ideal foundation from which to create, innovate and achieve. Compassion positively impacts creativity.

The vagus nerve bundle is connected to facial expression, which

---

[42] Cunningham, Anthony. *The Heart of What Matters: The Role for Literature in Moral Philosophy*. University of California, September 2001. Keltner, Dacher. "The Compassionate Instict". Greater Good Science Centre Website. Spring 2004. http://greatergood.berkeley.edu/article/item/the_compassionate_instinct/
[43] Rand, Ayn. *Faith and Force: The Destroyers of the Modern World*. Second Renaissance Press, June 1993.

might be why the mere act of smiling brings health benefits. Smiling counters the stress reaction, calms the heart, boosts immunity and lowers blood pressure as well as stimulates the release of endorphins (natural pain killers) and serotonin (influences mood and regulates the cardio vascular system). Go one step further to laugh and you'll get all the benefits of smiling plus additional ones related to improved circulation and respiration as well as exercise for your abdominals.

You don't even have to feel happy to reap the benefits of a smile. Cardiac psychologist Dr. Stephen Parker is one of many medical practitioners who note that even mimicking a smile, such as when you hold a pencil in your teeth, brings about the health benefits of smiling. Such benefits will improve your mood, in an example of how taking a physical action can elicit a desired emotion. Of course, those benefits are more significant when the smile is genuine. Contrast this with holding that pencil with your lips, which engages the facial muscles required for frowning, and you invoke the stress reaction. When Thich Nhat Hanh wrote "Sometimes your joy is the source of your smile, but sometimes your smile can be the source of your joy," he was teaching wisdom that science now validates.

In her talks, Cherokee scholar and activist Andrea Smith often urges us to have more fun at our demonstrations, conferences and events. Of course, she's not the only one who understands that having fun is an effective and enjoyable recruitment tool. It also mitigates against burnout and can decrease interpersonal tension. Improving health is a further benefit.

HeartMath states that the consequences of "positive" emotions include: enhanced physical and mental performance, enhanced creativity, innovative problem solving, more effective decision-making, a greater capacity for flexibility, improved memory and enhanced immunity.[44] In sum, cultivating feelings of compassion, gratitude, generosity, forgiveness, love, appreciation and other optimistic, pro-social states can play a significant role in maintaining a healthy relationship to self. The heart plays a crucial role in this process as does the brain.

---

[44] HeartMath, The Inside Story.

CHAPTER SIX: JEDI BRAIN TRICKS

Neuroscientist Alvaro Pascual-Leone once conducted some experiments at Harvard Medical School that imaged the brains of volunteers who had learned the piano. After a mere five days of practicing it was found that the volunteers' motor cortex, which controls finger movement, had grown. The brains of the participants had actually changed structurally to accommodate and facilitate the learning of a new skill.

Pascual-Leone's next move compared the brains of people who were *actually* learning to play the piano with people who only *thought* about playing. The "thinkers" held their hands still but imagined the movements they would make if actually playing the instrument. What Pascual-Leone found was that the areas of the brain responsible for controlling piano playing had expanded as much in the actual players as it had in those who had merely thought about playing. Mental practices alone created the same brain changes as the actual physical activity.[45] These, among other studies, have thoroughly upended theories about brain development and the brain's capacity to heal itself. Thus begins our review of some newish discoveries about the brain in our exploration of mind/body interaction.

The dominant science has long accepted the idea that your brain impacts how you think. Increasingly we are discovering the opposite, how much your thinking impacts and changes your brain. A changed brain reinforces the thinking that changed it and the whole process can become an upward cycle that some scientists refer to as a "brightening of the mind." This newly discovered process has implications for pretty much everything we have ever known about training, education, socialization, psychology, parenting, culture and so much more.

Brain "Tricks"

Let's start our brain tricks exploration by looking at the relationship

---

[45] "How the Brain Rewires Itself", Time Magazine. January 19, 2007. http://www.time.com/time/magazine/article/0,9171,1580438,00.html

between your feelings and your brain. Did you know that to engage in rational thinking and decision-making you must access the emotional centres of your brain? Academics usually love hearing this as they work in institutions that expect one to separate heart from mind; where rational thought is presumed to be devoid of feelings. But that is impossible. Human beings just aren't built that way. We know this in part from people who have had the emotional centres of their brains damaged by stroke or accident.

The Adult Brain: To Think by Feeling is a chapter in *The Secret Life of the Brain*, a film series by PBS. One of the stories in this chapter looks at a man who had the emotional centres of his brain damaged by a stroke. He became incapable of making the simplest of day-to-day decisions. From the time he got up in the morning until he went to bed at night he was unable to make a single choice for himself. He couldn't decide whether to shower, what to wear, what he wanted for breakfast and so on. His wife was making all those choices for him. What's the connection between feelings and decision-making?

What we now know about the relationship between thought and emotion is that if you cannot associate a feeling with a point of view, you can't formulate an opinion. If you can't associate a feeling with the outcome of a choice, you can't make that choice. For example, if you are faced with a decision to enroll in university and you can't anticipate how you might feel if you went to university and compare that with the feeling you anticipate if you didn't go, you can't make that decision. This doesn't mean that other factors aren't involved in the decision-making process but it's clear that feelings *must* be involved.

So the obvious question to ask yourself as an individual and certainly as an activist is, which emotions inform your philosophy, political opinions and actions? Is it anger and fear or love and compassion? The answer is obvious when we look at Tea Partiers. Their public image suggests they are motivated by fear and anger. But what about us social justice types? The question matters from the perspective of personal wellbeing as well as from the perspective of establishing healthy, sustainable movements and creating a socially just world.

What emotional states best serve the building of movements, the welcoming of new activists, and getting work done? Which emotional mindset best facilitates innovative, resilient and strategic thinking? What emotional energies are more likely to support useful discussions and coming to consensus as we co-create a better world?

Research conducted by Director Fox of the Affective Neuroscience Laboratory at the University of Essex (UK) shows that optimism and pessimism can impact our lives in significant ways. Optimists are more likely to enjoy higher paying jobs, stronger interpersonal relationships and better health than their pessimistic counterparts. Of particular interest to activists is that optimism correlates with heightened creativity.[46] So, it seems to me that optimism serves the cause of social justice.

Optimism is more than a cheery disposition and a denial or repression of anything uncomfortable. It's about maintaining an underlying sense of appreciation, seeing opportunities as well as focusing time and energy on positives over negatives.

Neuroplasticity

Do you have a genetic predisposition toward optimism or pessimism? There may be ways in which your brain is biased one way or the other, however, science is now clear: optimism and pessimism are not necessarily permanent mindsets.

When I was studying medical technology I learned that the adult brain was basically shaped for life. Consequently, changing habits or engrained, entrenched beliefs was either impossible or required Herculean efforts. Furthermore, people who had suffered brain injuries could never expect to regain function in damaged areas. For example, if the part of your brain responsible for walking was damaged, you would never walk again. Similarly if your speech centre was injured in an accident you would never talk again. I was taught that, unlike other cells in our body, when neurons died, they were gone forever and never replaced. Once synapses fell into disuse or were damaged, that connection was silenced forever. Our neural pathways, the grooves that form to facilitate habitual activities, were basically seen as carved in stone, deep and unchangeable.

Well, guess what? That's not true.

A child's physical, mental and emotional development would certainly be negatively impacted by trauma and neglect, as well as emotional or other types of abuse. Such experiences stunt neuronal (brain cell) growth, choke off synapses (communication connections between neurons), kill or reshape neurons (brain cells) and, inhibit integration between the right and left lobes of the brain. More recent findings demonstrate that abuse, trauma and even loneliness can do the same in the adult brain. In fact, major depression and chronic stress actually result in a loss of brain tissue as well as emotional and cognitive impairment. [47]

As usual, medical science more quickly picked up on the negative side of things than the positive. The good news is that stunted growth and

---

[46] Suttie, Jill. "Rainy Brain, Sunny Brain".
http://greatergood.berkeley.edu/article/item/rainy_brain_sunny_brain
[47] Mathaway, Bill. "Yale Team Discovers How Stress and Depression Can Shrink the Brain", August 12, 2012.
http://www.sciencenewsline.com/articles/2012081315270034.html

some other brain impairments do not have to be permanent.

Neuroplasticity is the science that looks at how "plastic," pliable and changeable the brain is. Neurons actually die and are born all the time. Synapses come and go constantly. Neural pathways, which connect one part of the brain to another, also shift and transform. The brain shapes and reshapes itself continuously as it learns and interacts with its environment, including ongoing changes provoked by our emotional states. Our brains are actually less like hardened stones and more like lumps of malleable clay. Every thought, feeling and experience you have changes your brain.

There are a growing number of brain injury cases showing that undamaged areas of this resilient organ can sometimes pick up the function of damaged ones. With the help of new therapeutic techniques stroke sufferers, for example, can sometimes regain lost brain functions.

The brain can be rewired! And, as we saw in the piano-learning example in the opening paragraphs of this chapter, thoughts alone can underwrite this process (provided your brain has enough nutrition, oxygen and other supports to function in healthy ways).

A University of Toronto study demonstrated that cognitive behavioural therapy (CBT), which looks at changing people's perceptions and feelings about their experiences, was more effective than drug treatments at alleviating depression. The August 2012 issue of *Nature Medicine* reported that CBT in this study changed the brains of 27 clinically depressed participants in ways that supported the new beliefs, perceptions and feelings they were working to internalize.[48]

Eighteen patients diagnosed with Obsessive Compulsive Disorder (OCD) engaged in ten weeks of mindfulness meditation in a study at the University of California. During the meditation they were instructed to observe their obsessive thoughts as though they were external to them; as though the thoughts belonged to someone else. Twelve of the 18 participants improved significantly. Scans revealed that the brains of those twelve had reshaped themselves to resemble the brains of people who had been treated with OCD medications.[49]

The Garrison Institute in New York studies and promotes mindfulness and meditation in schools. In 2004 the institute undertook a survey to determine how mindfulness was impacting school children. The results indicated that children who practiced mindfulness were less distracted, more focused and generally better learners. In one case, the introduction of mindfulness practices eliminated "behavioural problems" of students in a class that initially had the worst record in the school.[50]

---

[48] ibid.
[49] ibid.
[50] Suttie, Jill. "Mindful Kids, Peaceful Schools". Greater Good Science Centre.

The Mindfuness Based Stress Reduction (MBSR) Program at the University of Massachusetts Medical School was founded by Jon Kabat Zinn. This program has been found to reduce chronic pain, high blood pressure and cholesterol levels. The MBSR program at the Mindful Awareness Research Center at the University of California has improved the focus and mood of teenagers diagnosed with Attention Deficit Hyperactivity Disorder (ADHD).

Apparently, mindfulness, in and of itself, restructures the brain. The minute we pay attention to our thoughts or physical processes the brain begins reshaping itself in ways that bias us toward facilitating mindfulness. This type of mental training allows us to increase awareness of our thoughts and feelings, thus heightening our capacity to shift and change them if we so desire. The more we practice mindfulness the easier it is and the more engrained the structural changes become.

This is true of optimism, compassion, appreciation and any other thoughts we engage in. The more you think and feel these things, the more your brain is reshaped to intensify and prolong such thoughts and feelings. Thus, you can experience an upward cycle of "brain brightening." The expression, "brains that fire together wire together" is heard a lot in neuroplasticity circles. It basically means that the more you use specific parts of your brain, the stronger the connections become among the neurons responsible for that activity and the more your brain reshapes itself to facilitate that function. In fact, as we'll discuss in Shape-shifting Tricksters, we need only observe people being kind, caring and generous to benefit from brain changes that support positive shifts in our own behaviours.

Even more exciting, we now understand that expressions of love, caring concern, compassion, kindness, generosity, loving touch and so on, whether we're expressing these, are the recipients of them, or witness to them, can lead to high levels of right and left brain integration, as well as a lot of other positive effects on physical brain development: synapses multiply, healthy neurons form, blood flow to the brain improves, and so on. These changes are the result of feeling good but are also the objective, measurable indicators of optimum physical, mental and emotional health.

Of course, like anything else, the brain's capacity to rewire itself can have a downside. Negative thoughts, particularly when they become habitual, regular or obsessive will remold our brains to reinforce negativity as surely as positive thoughts reinforce positive restructuring.

Experts are not entirely sure of just how "plastic" the brain is and what the limits of neuroplasticity are. However, it is clear that much of

Summer 2007.
http://greatergood.berkeley.edu/article/item/mindful_kids_peaceful_schools/

what was once thought to be impossible years ago is, in fact, very possible. What's more each of us has the capacity to guide the direction of our brains' development.

Another piece of newish knowledge about brain function is the "use it or lose it" principal. Elders who once spoke their Native languages in childhood have experienced this. After having their language literally beaten out of them in the Indian Residential School System many survivors find they have forgotten most or all of their mother tongue. Just like the muscles in your body that will atrophy if you don't use them, you need to use functions of your brain in order to keep them.

This was not good news from my point of view because I've always believed I had a bad memory – a characteristic I was born with. Unfortunately for me, I can't claim that anymore. I have to face the fact that I've trained my brain to be lazy about remembering certain things. This is not the case with the Elders I refer to above who have the combination of colonial-authored trauma, combined with forced isolation from their communities, to thank for losing their language skills. Knowing all of this I am left with the highest admiration for those Elders who not only can remember their language but also manage to teach it to others. For those who don't remember, I can completely understand why and am nevertheless grateful that they survived their ordeals when so many others did not.

In any case, it is now clear that your neurons behave much like the other cells of your body, which shape and reshape themselves based, in part, on the bio-chemicals in your bloodstream. Thoughts and feelings play a role in regulating the bio-chemicals in your bloodstream and can influence a restructuring of your cells and organs, including your brain.

The types and amounts of bio-chemicals in your body fluids are determined, in part, by your conscious and subconscious thoughts and feelings. That isn't to say that genes, socialization and the physical environment don't matter. If you're not getting adequate nutrition or have been exposed to environmental toxins or are being harassed on the job, it's going to impact your brain. Injustices from the past and present will continue to impact your wellbeing. It's important to understand how the current system and past wrongs are impacting us. It's further helpful to work in communities so that injustice is minimized. It doesn't, however, make sense to contribute to a downward spiral of dysfunctionality for you and everyone around you by indulging in negative preoccupations. You can minimize the negative influences around you by focusing your thoughts and feelings on optimism and positivity whenever possible.

Healthy relationships with yourself and others are crucial to your wellbeing. Thoughts and feelings don't come out of nowhere. They come out of your relationships. They're responses to your physical, mental and emotional environment or your *perceived* environment. It's important to remember, however, that you aren't simply a victim. You can exert control over your thoughts and feelings, and can do so more and more with practice – whether that practice is intentional or not.

Cultivating positive emotions through managing your thoughts, remembering warm and fuzzy experiences, fantasizing about what you enjoy, or imagining a socially just world will positively impact your health. The more you do it, the easier it gets, as you restructure your physical body, including your brain, to switch to positive states faster, stay there longer and improve the quality of the experience.

By the way, it's never too late to reshape your brain. Research shows that people in their late 90's are still capable of benefiting health wise and in other ways from a shift in their thinking. Just as you can sculpt your muscles through exercise you can intentionally and purposefully, through mental and emotional exercise, reshape your brain to support your holistic wellbeing.

Indigenous peoples have known this for millennia, which is why prayers, ceremonies and teachings across cultures stress caring, sharing and thanksgiving. We and Our Relations benefit from this mindset in various ways.

An apt example is the Thanksgiving Address, spoken at all Haundenosaunee (Iroquois) gatherings. This address is normally given by an Elder who has committed it to memory in one of the Haundenosaunee languages (although you can find English translations online and in publications). It takes a long time to deliver this address – sometimes an hour or more. Why? Because time is taken to name and thank all of life for providing us two-leggeds with food, clothing, medicine, shelter, transportation, teachings – even entertainment. From the creepers and crawlers in the ground, to the swimmers, to the four-leggeds, to the flyers, to mountains, waters, oceans and wind, to the beings of the Sky World – Brother Sun, Grandmother Moon and Star Beings -- and finally the Great Spirit/Creator– everything is thanked for its role in keeping us human beings alive.

What Haundenosaunee people have known for generations is that reciting the Thanksgiving Address regularly provides an opportunity for speakers and listeners alike to feel and express gratitude, appreciation and compassion, thereby benefiting from physiological processes that generate wellbeing.

The Thanksgiving Address is only one practice that promotes health. There are similar practices in all indigenous cultures and many spiritual traditions around the world. Gratitude or compassion meditations are examples. Nowadays in North America meditation practices are often disassociated and separated from the spiritual and cultural contexts in which they evolved, so the social supports aren't always there; they aren't systemic. Yet these practices still impact us in positive ways. Dr. Joan Borysenko, medical scientist, psychologist and expert in stress health, talks about compassion, gratitude and altruism as being "core spiritualities" that can be practiced irrespective of religion. Whatever one's belief system, such feelings result in qualitative, measurable improvements in wellbeing.

In the literature, there tends to be a "four pillar" approach to brain health. Nutrition, physical exercise, stress management and mental stimulation are the "pillars" crucial to maintaining brain wellness over a lifetime. This reminds us that managing thoughts and feelings are not a substitute for other ways of ensuring brain health but are part of a many-pronged strategy.

As an activist, however, it makes me wonder what happens to people who don't have access to healthy food and cannot manage all their stressors because their social locations leave them with limited power to do so. This is what survivors of residential schools experienced as children. It's hard to imagine that malnourished and abused children or people living in war torn regions or those drinking contaminated waters can manage their brain and other forms of health by simply refocusing their thoughts and feelings. That's one of many reasons why activism is important.

I shouldn't think we need hard science to prove that the stresses of poverty, racism and other forms of political, economic and social oppressions negatively impact our brain health. If individuals and whole groups of people are prohibited from achieving optimum brain health the rest of society is deprived of their potential creativity, innovation and other contributions. If there's one thing the world needs in great quantities at this juncture, it's creativity and innovation.

The cultures of poverty, consumerism and settler colonialism have seriously unhealthy consequences for all of us. A very new area of research in neuroplasticity relates to how culture wires and rewires the brain.

Cultural Neuroscience

Cultural neuroscience might be of interest to social justice advocates who are concerned with issues like racism, colonialism and other forms of social inequality. This area of study might provide us with a stronger case to demonstrate the existence, impact and consequences of systemic "isms". Such information relates strongly to what we discussed when looking at worldviews and paradigms. For example, if you have been socialized in a culture that values healthy relationships, humility, and cooperation your brain will be wired quite differently from someone who was raised in a context where individualism and competition are prized. Naturally, there are many consequences of this.

To give a very simple example, culture shapes how the brain

responds to and interprets body language. The hand sign for "OK" in North America looks very much like the gesture for "I swear/promise" in Nicaragua. Both of these meanings would be processed differently in the brain.[51] A Canadian traveling in Nicaragua who became aware of this would undergo a bit of brain rewiring in order to first of all, differentiate the two similar gestures and, secondly, associate the new gesture with its meaning in the Nicaraguan cultural environment.

But this research has deeper implications. For instance psychologists have found that what lights up a specific part of the brain in people living in the United States is different from what lights up that same brain area for people living in China. For American participants in one study, adjectives used to describe them activated a different part of the brain than adjectives applied to family members. For Chinese participants, however, adjectives used to describe both participants and family members lit up the same brain area; their brains did not differentiate whether the adjective was being applied to them or their relatives. Psychologists conducting the study noted that cultural understandings and beliefs about how we relate to others were responsible for this difference.[52]

Similarly, research undertaken by psychologists Shinobu Kitayama at the University of Michigan and Denise C. Park at the University of Texas show that, in terms of interpreting, describing and ascribing meaning to visual images, Asians paid more attention to context while Americans paid more attention to details.[53] One might see this as the relational versus reductionist mindset at work. However, the issue is much more complex than concluding that culture shapes the brain in such a linear fashion.

To illustrate, Tufts psychologist Nailini Ambady found different responses from Americans and Japanese participants looking at silhouettes characterized as "dominant" (standing tall and straight, arms crossed, for example) and "submissive" (head bowed, shoulders rounded). In Americans the "dominant" images provoked a reaction in the brain's reward circuit unlike the "submissive" ones. In Japanese participants the reward circuit activated with "submissive" images and not with the

[51] CBC News. "Culture shapes how brain interprets signals". July 18, 2007. http://www.cbc.ca/news/technology/story/2007/07/18/science-gesture.html

[52] Meyer, Megan, PhD Student. "How Culture Shapes Our Mind and Brain". Brain Blogger. http://brainblogger.com/2009/10/10/how-culture-shapes-our-mind-and-brain/

[53] Lende, Daniel. "Cultural Neuroscience – Culture and the Brain". Public Library of Science website. June 22, 2012. http://blogs.plos.org/neuroanthropology/2010/11/26/cultural-neuroscience-%E2%80%93-culture-and-the-brain/

"dominant" ones. The differing responses were attributed to differing cultural values, i.e., American's value control more than the Japanese.[54] In reading about this study I had difficulty with the word "submissive" and the implications that Japanese folks are more likely to value submissiveness and obedience to authority. Here we see how one's scientific paradigm impacts assumptions and interpretations, in this case perpetuating a racial stereotype. Where people trained in mainstream science might see submissiveness in a bowed head or rounded shoulders, others of us might see the body language of honour and respect, an act of humility or someone in prayer. The pleasure centres of those who value those activities and states of mind might light up upon seeing them. This demonstrates again how worldviews and paradigms impact how we think, what we sense and what we don't, as well as how we *interpret* what we sense.

Even scientists involved in the experiments above caution us about using their research to generalize about people affiliated with or socialized within specific cultures and/or to justify valuing one culture over another. Northwestern University's Joan Chiao, for example, found no cultural consistency could be found when a group representative of many ethno-racial backgrounds was tested on their brain responses to honesty. However, when she assessed participants according to whether they valued collectivism or individualism, she found that collectivists had the same brain reaction to the adjective honest whether it was used in relation to themselves or their mothers. Individualists did not. The cultural background of the participants was irrelevant; it was their *values* that mattered.[55] Ethno-culture passes on values but today most people are exposed to many cultural influences, most significantly those of consumerism, individualism and materialism.

While it's true that culture is not the only relevant part of our social location that impacts our values and our brain development, my main point in sharing these very preliminary findings in a new area of study is to simply raise awareness of how culture, values and brain development (and probably many other factors) can interact. Like everything we've discussed above, there are both positive and negative applications for this information. To illustrate, we might use such information to demonstrate how

[54] ibid.
[55] Azar, Beth. "Your Brain on Culture", American Psychological Association Website. November 2010, Vol 41, No. 10, Print version: page 44
http://www.apa.org/monitor/2010/11/neuroscience.aspx

harmful the monoculture of capitalism, consumerism and competition can be. Take TV-watching, for instance. It takes only a few minutes (5-15) for anyone watching a television program to find themselves in a Theta-wave brain state. In this state, which we'll discuss more thoroughly in Shape-shifting Tricksters, you're in a very suggestible mindset. So the values that underlie what you're watching (which include messages like "police protect you," "buying stuff makes you happy," and "whiteness is beautiful") are speaking directly to your subconscious. What happens if your subconscious has already been programmed with cultural values that contradict the new information? What happens if your cultural programming was contradictory to begin with? What if your experiences belie the message? What happens when information we receive from popular culture reinforces values that don't serve a socially just world? How is your brain being reshaped and restructured with these new messages? What are the outcomes for you, your family and communities?

I haven't looked at hard science research that specifically addresses these questions (if there is any out there) but we can find some answers in our cultural environment. There are enough sales of dangerous skin whiteners and hair straighteners to keep a variety of companies in business all over the world, demonstrating how many have internalized the "white is beautiful" message. Environmental devastation and workplace injuries (not to mention deaths) caused by mining for gold, diamonds and other luxury items demonstrate how popular culture has created a market for status symbols to showcase the wealth and power some people believe makes them happy. The lack of police accountability in our society, which empowers authorities to destroy lives and even get away with murder, reinforces the case that mainstream media can play a role in skewing our perceptions of who protects whom from what.

A more dangerous question being asked by mainstream science is: if culture shapes biology, how does biology shape culture? From a relational point of view the bio-determinism and reductionism inherent in that question is a bit unsettling, as it may not leave open the possibility that there are many, many influences on both culture and biology; that culture and biology interact with each other as well as a vast array of phenomenon such as the lands we live on, cosmic electro-magnetism, seasonal rhythms of the Earth and so on. It leaves some of us wondering whether the science will be used to judge some cultures as "backward", "primitive" or in the way of progress, which is what some hard and soft science has already concluded. In any case, we'll see in the next chapter on Intersecting Force Fields that ideas about biology and culture being in relationship with each other as well as our physical environment are far from superstitious nonsense or untenable ideas from science fiction.

Nevertheless, as we collect information on the inter-relationality of culture and brain development can we use it in ways that support social justice and wellbeing rather than in ways that manipulate, confuse and exploit people? Can we do the same with neuroscience? I would argue, yes, provided we do so within the framework of relationality and not linear, reductionist materialism. Even further, I suggest that studying these within the framework of relationality is more likely to provide us with comprehensive information that will support the creation of a socially just world.

Other issues related to brain tricks have to do with the interaction of individuals and communities. The next chapter speaks to how some of the phenomena we've discussed so far can't simply be understood within the framework of individual wellbeing and development. Everything about us as individuals impacts other living beings (just as they impact us) whether we're conscious of it or not.

CHAPTER SEVEN: INTERSECTING FORCE FIELDS

While it's readily evident how the science we've discussed so far relates to self-care, it is equally relevant to community care. Obviously, individual wellbeing relates to community wellbeing. In this chapter we'll discuss how self-care specifically impacts others in our networks. We'll also explore our more direct energetic connections to each other as human beings, as well as to other life on the planet. All life emits energy fields that interact with each other. We are entangled in each other's spirits, our energy fields intersect, whether we are aware of it or not.

Just as we've been seeing throughout, the dominant science has long recognized the health impacts of negativity on individuals. This is similarly true in terms of social relationships. Abusive and dysfunctional relationships as well as social deprivation negatively impact our physical, emotional and mental development. When anger, hatred or sadness motivate another's actions towards you, you will be negatively impacted. This is best understood at the material/physical level. As we know, there are many forms of violent, threatening and aggressive behavior that impact the person behaving badly, the target of the abuse, and even witnesses. This is why, for example, children who witness domestic violence, even if they themselves are not targeted by it, are traumatized and consequently at higher risk to either become abusers or be abused in their own relationships. This is knowledge that violence prevention agencies, women's shelters and health care centres all over the world struggle to make common knowledge.

Increasingly, we have come to understand that neglect and isolation also cause harm. The detrimental effects of withholding affection, caring touch and other types of loving, physical contact has been known for some time. We learned decades ago that infants who aren't cuddled, touched lovingly, and caressed on a regular basis suffer developmentally: physically, mentally and emotionally. This is the case even when all of their other physical needs are looked after. Consequently, hospitals often recruit volunteers to hold, cuddle and caress infants whose parents are unable to do so.

Loneliness is an area that is increasingly being studied as it also has a detrimental impact on our physical and mental health. Feeling lonely is now understood to influence and contribute to clinical depression and other forms of stress. Enforced isolation, such as solitary confinement in prisons, does the same. Along with that stress comes a much higher risk for all the forms of illness and mental impairments discussed previously. High blood pressure, shingles and eczema are but a few of the specific diseases linked to stress. Hence, being deprived of or isolated by circumstance from meaningful relationships with others is a health hazard. Bottom line: if loneliness isn't recognized and dealt with, it can kill. This is why many prisoner rights advocates have campaigned to have solitary confinement officially recognized as a form of torture and a human rights violation.

Not surprisingly, the negative impacts of unhealthy relationships were discovered first. Now, hard science is increasingly showing us the positive impact of respectful, intimate, and caring social relationships. The work isn't only about relationships among two-leggeds. There has also been research on relationships across species. Life impacts life in physical, emotional, mental *and* spiritual/energetic ways. Science is increasingly able to measure and quantify some of that.

Self-Compassion

The role that self-compassion plays in wellbeing, achievement and connection has been a focus of scientific inquiry for Dr. Kristin Neff, Associate Professor in Human Development and Culture at the University of Texas. Neff argues that *self*-compassion is as important to cultivate as compassion for others. In fact, her work illustrates how they are connected.

Self-compassion should not be confused with self-pity, Neff emphasizes, which involves becoming so immersed in your own problems that you forget about those of others. "Self-pity," she writes, "tends to emphasize egocentric feelings of separation from others and exaggerate the extent of personal suffering."[56]

According to Neff there are three components to self compassion: 1) self kindness, especially when we make mistakes, 2) feeling a sense of connectedness or common humanity; acknowledging that we are not alone in our troubles and that challenges are a part of the human experience and, 3) acknowledging our suffering in a way that neither dismisses nor blows our situation out of proportion.

Psychologists have fallen out of love with the concept of self-esteem, Neff claims, preferring the notion of self-compassion. Why? She notes that in the dominant culture it's not okay to be average. People need to feel above average, must stand out, must be a cut above, in order to feel good about themselves. We feel less than adequate if we are not richer than, prettier than, or smarter than. Dominant cultural values encourage us

---

[56] Neff, Kristin. Selfcompassion.org: http://www.self-compassion.org/

to always compare ourselves to others.[57] If we are found to be lacking in some way the inevitable remedy is to spend money on a product or service to improve our perceived inadequacy in relation to a, usually, unattainable standard.

Neff notes that bullies are among those that score well on self-esteem assessments, due to something she labels as the "better than" effect. In other words, to feel good about yourself you must feel superior to others in some way. Feelings of narcissism, isolation, and superiority can correlate with having high self-esteem. I wonder whether this form of self-esteem can lead to the need to put down, devalue and obstruct others and their contributions because they are seen as threatening to that perceived superiority. Case in point is how Indigenous agricultural communities were prohibited by the *Gradual Civilization Act of 1857* from selling their produce at markets in the Toronto area because White farmers felt they had an unfair advantage.[58] The Jim Crow laws, which mandated segregation between African-descended people and Whites in the US is another example. In both cases, Whites felt they had to sabotage the survival of other peoples in order to protect their myth of White supremacy. Whites responsible for enacting and benefitting from these laws, clearly felt inferior to others or they would have no need of such legislation. It is such legislation and other acts of obstructing the development of other communities that form the basis of imagined White supremacy as well as all the privilege Whites enjoy in our societies to this day.

In sum, Neff notes, self-esteem involves judging or evaluating oneself positively whereas self-compassion has nothing to do with judging or evaluation. It's about having a balanced way of relating to yourself with kindness and an awareness of your and other people's suffering. You care for yourself the way you care for others, recognizing that just being human is enough to be worthy of such consideration. Self-compassion, Neff says, has all of the benefits of self-esteem with none of its drawbacks.

We can logically assume self-compassion also has the same biochemistry and physiology as HRV Coherence. Feelings, words and actions reflecting self-compassion are known to generate the secretion of oxytocin and activate the vagus nerve, with all the positive physical, mental and emotional affects these physiological processes produce.

Neff's work shows that people in care-taking fields like nursing or personal caregivers are less likely to experience compassion fatigue if they score high on self-compassion assessments. Compassion fatigue is a feeling of burnout or exhaustion as a result of continually caring for others. But

---

[57] ibid.
[58] Sanderson, Frances and Howard-Bobiwash, Heather. *The Meeting Place: Aboriginal Life in Toronto*. Native Canadian Centre. 1997. Page 19.

self-compassionate people seem to have deeper reserves and a greater capacity to renew themselves while caregiving. Neff also says there is some evidence suggesting that self-compassionate people fare better in intimate relationships like marriages. Being better able to attend to their own emotional needs they are less controlling, less manipulative and more able to give from a heartfelt place.

It's easy to see that self-compassion offers an example of how your perception of yourself impacts others in your life. Such studies on self-compassion are of particular interest to activists. How many times have you felt guilty or ashamed of not doing enough? How many times have you chided yourself for enjoying or lacking awareness of white-skinned/light-skinned privilege? Heterosexual privilege? First World privilege? Or for making mistakes? How many times have you compared yourself to historical figures, role models or other activists and judged yourself as better or worse in some way?

What would self-compassion look like for an activist? Might it mean reminding yourself from time to time that being an activist is not easy? That mistakes are learning opportunities, even if they feel terrible in the moment? That all of us experience guilt and shame from time to time? That everyone runs out of energy, feels depressed and gets disappointed? Maybe when you are feeling sad, frustrated or just plain terrified it might help to remember that those feelings better enable you to understand another's pain and suffering and make a compassionate connection.

A blog story written by a young man who had been arrested during the G20 Summit protests of June 2011 in Toronto might demonstrate the value of cultivating internal reserves. All weekend long demonstrators who had been, in most cases, unjustly arrested and had their civil rights violated were locked up in a filthy, makeshift prison where they were kept in over-crowded conditions, denied medical attention, refused adequate food and water as well as, in some cases, sexually and physically assaulted.[59] In this story the young man, who identified as White, described how his cellmates spent their twenty plus hours in lock-up. They complained about the facilities, protested the violation of their rights, asked for lawyers, demanded food or drink and pleaded for bathroom access. The one man in

---

[59] Some, among many sources, reporting on this include the Toronto Star: http://www.thestar.com/news/gta/article/1197157--g20-senior-commander-facing-misconduct-charges-for-ordering-u-of-t-mass-arrest, http://www.thestar.com/news/gta/torontog20summit/article/1180052--g20-aftermath-high-ranking-and-frontline-toronto-police-officers-face-charges, http://www.thestar.com/news/gta/crime/article/1258153--g20-fallout-police-boards-association-agrees-with-report-calling-for-stronger-oversight and http://www.thestar.com/news/gta/torontog20summit/article/1229148--g20-oversight-police-chair-apologizes-to-innocent-people-for-what-they-suffered

the cell who did not engage in this behaviour was described as "Native." He was thought to be complacent, bored and possibly used to being arrested and mistreated by police. In the story he sat calmly and quietly, urging his agitated cellmates to play games and chill out.

As I read the story I suspected the behaviours attributed to the Native man were not about complacency or boredom, but patience, groundedness and dignity. From this foundation he was able to entertain, distract and lighten the mood of his otherwise anxious cellmates. To me, this is an example of how possessing a calm inner reserve can help others. Self-compassion, according to Neff's research, is one way of cultivating this "internal reserve".

How would self-compassion translate into a collective setting? If our groups practiced collective self-compassion would we be less threatened by copping to mistakes or failures? Would we be more likely to forgive, absorb the lessons and move on? How would self-compassionate assessment of our work look in relation to practices that we now employ to ensure accountability and effectiveness? How would collective self-compassion impact our relationships with other activist communities?

While some might bristle at the idea that activists should spend an inordinate amount of time navel-gazing or centering activist issues in the struggle, I maintain that self-compassion would increase our effectiveness and impact. I further wonder how much the resistance to deep self-reflection I've observed in activist circles is based in colonial, left-brained values. The so-called "Protestant work ethic" tells us that blood, sweat and tears will earn us a ticket to heaven in the afterlife. While many activists, Christian or not, reject this, some still behave in ways that suggest that collective reflection and periods of stillness are unproductive ways of spending time. Or maybe our individual demons urge constant movement so we don't have to feel and deal with personal pain (which is one example of how personal pain is also a social issue).

Though activism is defined in part by taking action, it shouldn't be the only aspect of our work that is valued. We can give ourselves permission to be still and reflect, even if it means feeling uncomfortable sometimes. As individuals and groups we could take responsibility to just *be* instead of constantly meeting, planning and "taking action." We could stop repressing our personal or collective feelings and dismissing them as less important than alleviating injustice as quickly as possible. How is it exactly that stressed out activists, perpetually in fight/flight/freeze states, are going to usher peace and justice into the world anyway?

As we know, sleep is essential to wellbeing. Winter and dry seasons allow life on the Earth to rest and go dormant for a while. These natural cycles serve the ongoing regeneration of life. Our emotions are also cyclical and rhythmic and those patterns serve a purpose.

British physicist Geoffrey Brian West is best known for theorizing about the issue of scaling in biology, from the molecular level to organisms to ecosystems. He theorizes that the math of biological scaling is equally applicable to human organizations such as corporations, institutions and cities. I don't know what West's relationship is to social justice but he has shown, both mathematically and in the real world, that organisms experience similar birth, growth, stabilization and death cycles. All of life has the same metabolic to body mass ratio (which casts some doubt for me on the random mutation theory of Darwinist evolution, but I digress). Furthermore, large or small, all organisms benefit from an economy of scale where, with a doubling in size, we do *not* require a doubling of energy inputs but only an increase of 75%. The bigger you get the less oxygen, nourishment and other inputs each of the cells of your body need per capita. This is one example of the economy of scale principle, which holds that organized growth is efficient in that it requires fewer per capita inputs. In addition, your metabolism slows as you increase in size – again, a principle applicable to individual organisms that grow from small to large as well as across smaller to larger species. For example, the metabolism of a 15-year-old is faster than that of her grandfather. The metabolism of a mouse is faster than that of an elephant.

These processes are common to all life forms in the natural world and even apply to communities or networks of life forms. Ant colonies, bee hives and lion prides benefit from economies of scale too. So do forests and ecosystems. The reason is because living entities form networks, specialize their roles, and work together for the benefit of the whole. In other words, they cooperate to be more efficient, whether they are cells in a body or individual organisms in a community.

When nature's communities get too big to benefit from economies of scale, they either die or split up to form new communities. This happens in beehives, ant colonies and other forms of animal networks. It used to happen in pre-colonial Indigenous societies as well, where decisions to relocate and possibly even split up would be made on the basis of whether communities were sustainable in relation to the land and resources upon which they relied. As Elder, educator and activist Robert Lovelace notes, "In nature, cells that grow beyond their ecological function and consume more than they produce are called cancer and this is not the norm."[60] However, when it comes to modern human communities, specifically urbanization, West's work shows us that doubling the population of a city

---

[60] Lovelace, Robert. "Foretelling the Future: Philosophical Discussions of Witchcraft and Culture" Lecture Notes. Used with permission. Former Co-Chief of the Ardoch Algonquin First Nation, Lovelace is an Elder, educator, author and activist.

actually *increases* the per capita amount of inputs and outputs required to maintain it. Human cities that double in size do not benefit from economies of scale; instead, they require a 15% per capita *increase* in energy, transportation activity, sewage infrastructure, food and so on. Waste, crime rates, the number of police, as well as the incidence of HIV/AIDS and flu also increase by a per capita rate of 15%. Doubling the size of a city also increases incomes, wealth, the number of patents that get filed, the number of colleges and so on by the same per capita percentage. This is true the world over, regardless of the city. The data is consistent whether we're talking about Tokyo, Sao Paolo, Kinshasa, Los Angeles or London. There are no economies of scale in a city.

In addition, West has found that walking speed also increases substantially with a city's population expansion, which is one of the indicators he uses to demonstrate that cities speed up our lives. Speed of life in urban settings is a parallel to the concept of metabolism in living organisms. West's theory suggests that our speedy pace of life might soon exceed human capacity. It certainly can be argued that speed sometimes deteriorates the quality of life because it doesn't allow us opportunity to take time to enjoy the present moment or notice details that are important to our activities. West also raises the question of urban sustainability in terms of whether resources will keep pace with our exponential rates of expansion. He notes that cities have collapsed for such reasons in the past, although many cities in history have saved themselves from crashing and burning because of the capacity for human innovation.

West's calculations validate the assertions of Indigenous leaders, environmentalists and social scientists alike, who conclude that our processes of urbanization as well as other aspects of the capitalist lifestyle, are not sustainable. They will collapse. West's mathematics extrapolates a range of dates for this to occur, based on our current social behaviours, although he doesn't ignore the possibility that human innovation and creativity can invalidate the numbers. He asserts that innovation and creativity could potentially, according to the math, save the world's cities. However, he also notes that such technological and other innovations would have to occur at an increasing rate of speed in a race against running out of resources and he's not sure the human organism has the capacity. Indigenous leaders suspect that Mother Earth's body lacks the capacity to feed our voracious appetites for meaningless stuff as well as for the types of innovations that further jeopardize the ongoing existence of many, many life forms crucial to our survival.

I wonder if West's work has implications for social justice activism? I've had occasion to work with groups that set impossible standards for their members in terms of the speed and intensity with which "the work" must get done. We do it to ourselves, normalizing a pace that suggests we are responding to an ongoing state of crisis. While I admit there are many, many crises in the world, I'm not sure that getting stuck in a crisis response as a group is any healthier than getting stuck as an individual in fight/flight/freeze. Organizations burn their members out and inherently set up conditions that generate conflict and unhealthy interpersonal dynamics. We find such expectations unacceptable to those who work in business and public institutions but somehow tolerate them in our activist organizations. It's impossible for activists to develop healthy relationships to one another if they don't give themselves time. Anyone in a life partnership can tell you that a good relationship requires an investment of time and energy. Constantly working or fusing work with play is hardly role modeling the socially just world we aspire to create.

Furthermore, it's impossible to accurately and compassionately assess your group's effectiveness in a context where you don't get an opportunity to stop, collect information, review and reflect. If you don't assess the impact of your work, you risk being ineffective as well as unwell (individually and as a group). Particularly when working in urban environments, we internalize the speedy pace of life and accept the assertion that busyness equals effectiveness and productivity. Unfortunately, I've worked and interacted with activist groups that have yet to deal with the issue of sustainability in any serious way.

Besides enabling an assessment of our work, slowing down allows us to enjoy the journey, to spend some time consciously appreciating and feeling the quality of our lives.

Elders have told me that taking the time to acknowledge, respond to and just *feel* our feelings – all of them – is essential to physical health. They remind me that feelings are responses to our relationships; past, present and future; to ourselves, our families and our communities, as understood in the broadest terms that include animal, plant and other life forms including the Earth Herself. Healing ceremonies are all about processing feelings. As discussed above, when we block and deny feelings we don't want to experience they persist, become stronger and manifest in unexpected, unwanted ways. Unacknowledged, denied and repressed feelings take a physical toll on us that can show up as illness, forcing us to slow down or stop altogether. I'm not entirely sure that negative feelings are the only ones we repress. How many times have you curtailed your positive emotional reaction because you judged it inappropriate to the context or because you had to get back to work? That can't be good for your personal wellbeing or your organization.

Clearly, activists need to practice self-compassion, individually and collectively, in order to be effective and useful. Certainly, we also need to be careful to not interpret the scientific findings discussed in this book in such a way that suggests that denial, repression and rejection of our feelings is in any way healthy or conducive to social justice.

At the same time, it would do some activists (and those of us that have to work with them) a world of good if they recalled that feeling separate, unconnected and superior in some way is what got our world into the mess it's in. We've all encountered egotistical and narcissistic leaders or people who role model arrogant, unfeeling and insensitive leadership styles. Clearly, that is not good for our movements.

After I published my first (and only) science fiction novel in 1998, I began outlining a second. A premise of this story was that humans had made contact with an alien race but every time we tried to approach this race, people killed themselves. Of course, Earth authorities and experts suspected the aliens were somehow behind the suicides, their ultimate aim to wipe out the human race by its own hand. However, as the story progresses you find out that this alien race is completely empathic and cannot so much as contemplate harming another being. They exist solely to bring joy and peace to others. So what was killing those who tried to make contact? In the end, we learn that the alien's empathy was actually contagious and when humans caught it they became severely despondent at recalling their personal and collective histories, particularly the misery and pain they had inflicted on each other, the Earth and Her children. This despondence led them to commit suicide as the ultimate act of sacrifice to save the universe from the harm humans could and would inevitably wreak.

I never published that story but always console myself by believing that the idea had some merit. The truth is, however, that we humans don't need to catch empathy from an alien race. Most of us are born with both the hardware and software to run an *empathy program* and, like all of our emotions, it is, in fact, contagious. More and more scientists are becoming convinced that empathy failures are the result of brain impairment, which can have physical or social origins.[61] Such brain impairments are behind behaviours like bullying. They are probably behind a lot of anti-social activities. If the science is right, a lot of people in our society suffer from some sort of brain impairment.

A study described in a *Science Daily* article from 2008 saw children responding empathically to the physical and emotional suffering of others depicted in animation. Suffering that resulted from accidents activated the children's empathy circuit, including the brain's mirroring reaction described earlier. Suffering that was the result of the deliberate, intentional actions, such as someone tripping another or harming them in some way, elicited the empathetic response but also activated the parts of the brain responsible for moral reasoning and social interaction. Comments made by

---

[61] Science Daily. "Children are Naturally Prone to be Empathetic and Moral". July 12, 2008. http://www.sciencedaily.com/releases/2008/07/080711080957.htm

the children in these instances indicated they were aware that an injustice had occurred.[62]

The questions for many researchers in light of this and other studies are: how does the empathy reaction that children experience get turned off or limited in adulthood? What are the implications? Dr. Dascher Keltner may be one of several scientists that can provide some answers.

Firstly, in terms of the difference between empathy and compassion, definitions in the literature differ and it's the desire to take action that is most often associated with compassion rather than empathy. However, within my reading of the hard science, it's not clear that there is a difference at all as both empathy and compassion activate the part of the brain that plans action. So it's possible that, in English at least, we are using two words to describe essentially the same emotion.

Keltner, who has been studying empathy, has come up with a term called "power paradox." In sum, the idea describes a phenomenon where groups generally select socially intelligent leaders, that is, people who can foster a sense of connection, understand and advance the goals of others as well as recognize and respond appropriately to other people's emotional states. The socially intelligent demonstrate skill at negotiating, reconciling conflict and smoothing over tension. The paradox occurs when such individuals get into positions of power, at which time their pro-social skill levels decline and their behaviours become less empathetic and compassionate.

The definition of power that Keltner prefers is less about violence, coercion and wealth than about the ability to significantly impact a person's life by providing or withholding resources such as money, knowledge, food and even affection as well as by administering consequences such as physical harm, job termination or social ostracism.

This definition allows you to consider how power dynamics operate in many areas of your life, including as an activist. We all know that activists are certainly not above using affection, knowledge and social ostracism as tools of manipulation. You don't have to be a general, a corporate magnate, or a prime minister to enjoy, use and abuse power. The notion that power differences in some situations are useful and necessary is a question that I haven't seen Keltner's work speak to directly. For example, parents have life and death power over their children and without that children wouldn't survive. The parent/child power dynamic when wielded in positive ways allows children to develop self-discipline and boundaries. For instance, I always tried to ensure as much as possible that my children suffered the consequences of their poor choices. If they drew

---

[62] Ibid.

on the walls they had to clean them. I had the power to ground them, withdraw TV and inflict other consequences not to manipulate but to allow them to experience real world-like consequences for their actions. It wasn't about punishment it was about helping them learn to make better choices in their lives. This is the theory I worked from but I certainly have to admit I lost my temper from time to time and was known to inflict unfair consequences on my kids though I *never* hit them or used other forms of violence. The closest I may have come to this was in physically restraining them for brief moments to keep them from things like running into a street full or cars or sticking their fingers in electrical sockets. So in this case the power I enjoyed as a mom came with huge responsibilities and ensured my sons' survival and development into adulthood. The point here is that even those of us at the bottom of the social hierarchy can and do enjoy some level of power during our lifetime. The question we need to ask ourselves is, are we wielding that power responsibly, with compassion and empathy, motivated by the wellbeing of others?

Keltner's work suggests that the popular notion that leaders get into positions of power through manipulation, control, or violence is not entirely accurate. It is actually good inter-personal skills and positive social engagement that involves serving, helping and caring for others that initially get people into positions of power. This is presumably because we're wired for sociability and cooperation in order to survive. Modesty and humility have also been identified as qualities that help people acquire and maintain power.

Yet Italian philosopher Niccolo Machiavelli's writings, which emphasize dishonesty, manipulation, ruthlessness and even terror have been seen in Eurocentric political culture as the gold standard of how to acquire and maintain power. This is not so in many other cultures. Confucianism and Taoism, for instance, extol humble models of leadership. "To lead the people, walk behind them," Lao-Tzu wrote.[63]

One teaching I received from the Haundenosaunee explains why the Hoyaneh (male leadership appointed by the Clan Mothers) wear deer antlers on their Gustoweh (headdress). Their role, I was told, is to stay abreast of what the community needs and wants so they can provide it. The antlers are a kind of symbolic antenna for leaders whose primary responsibility is to serve people not "rule over" them. Leadership, in this sense, is a responsibility and an honour, not an opportunity to wage war, lie and enrich oneself. The Clan Mothers who had watched these leaders grow from boys to men in small communities had the power to sack them when they were not honourably serving the people. Hence the warning I've

---

[63] http://thinkexist.com/quotation/to_lead_the_people-walk_behind_them/148373.html

heard Haundenosaunee women sometimes utter to men who become too self-centred or insensitive to community needs, "watch your horns," referring to the headdress of leadership, which can be taken away along with the trust of the people.

Folks who use Machiavellian techniques to win contests of power are actually seen by the vast majority for who they are, Keltner maintains, and, if people have the choice, such self-serving manipulators are not chosen for leadership positions. Keltner's work (and other's) shows that people or groups that attempt to seize power through some form of "muscle" don't last long in their positions because they don't have the support of the majority of the people and are soon toppled.

This might be true in some historical circumstances but I question this assertion when it comes to looking at colonization, for example. The power of Europeans who came to this continent was fundamentally based in vast their numbers (particularly after their diseases had time to depopulate Indigenous communities) as well as the brutal terror they waged with their superior weaponry. Colonization as an abusive form of power worked quite nicely for European settlers who democratically chose White supremacists, patriarchs and genocidists as their leaders for centuries. Electioneering leaders may have been very pro-social within their White communities. Meanwhile, Indigenous, African-descended and Asian communities disproportionately suffered deadly abuses of power. In the Americas, Machiavellianism has informed leadership for over 500 years. So I'd be careful with Keltner's conclusions on this count.

In any case, what studies have shown is that once leaders get into positions of power their social intelligence and empathetic responses tend to decline. In other words, these leaders fail to recognize and respond empathically and compassionately to other people. So British historian John Dalberg-Acton got it right when he asserted that, "Power tends to corrupt; absolute power corrupts absolutely." It is only the rare leader who maintains pro-social skills and consequently stays in power because they are perceived as fair and just.[64]

Whatever his political science theories, Keltner's conclusion is that power decreases social intelligence and the capacity to empathize. This happens in all social groups: street gangs, sports teams, parliament, congress and even activist groups.[65] It is certainly an issue in First Nations communities, as Robert Lovelace illustrates:

---

[64] Keltner. The Power Paradox.

[65] It's not clear from my readings of Keltner's work whether he has studied or come to conclusions around how accountability impacts the power paradox. Nor are the causes of power paradox entirely clear.

A student recently asked a colleague of mine, how you can tell when a person is an Elder. My colleague took that long breath hoping to find a rational answer. I inserted before the empty exhale had finished, "It is how they get in and out of a canoe". My colleague was relieved but as baffled as the student at my sideways reply. I have spent the better part of my life with an Elder, Harold Perry. When it comes down to it, it is simply how he gets in and out of his canoe. He is respectful of the canoe because it will need to last a long time. He is respectful of the gear in the canoe because he will need to use it. He is respectful of the others in the canoe because his relations with them are important. He is respectful of the place where he lands the canoe so that he does not disturb or upset the balance of things that are independent of his comings and goings. ... As Indigenous people we are in a vacancy of leadership. Many of us have forgotten how to get in and out of a canoe. There are many reasons why we are adrift and I am not going through the list. We all know the history of cause and effect. More over, it is the obsession with this history that is helping us to win the race to the bottom.[66]

The power paradox was seemingly demonstrated in 1971 with the infamous Stanford Prison Experiment. Psychologist Philip Zimbardo arranged for 24 students, chosen because they were in good physical and psychological health (and without criminal records) to simulate prisoner/prison guard relationships in the basement of a university building. "Guards" worked eight-hour shifts and were allowed to leave the premises when they weren't "on duty." "Prisoners", on the other hand, were locked up in the makeshift facility (which included an Isolation Room) 24 hours a day, seven days a week for the duration of the experiment. Student interactions were observed on hidden cameras. The planned 14-day experiment was called off after only six days when the abuse exacted by "guards" left "prisoners" showing signs of extreme stress and anxiety. Unfortunately, the widespread knowledge of the results of this experiment hasn't influenced greater accountability or any other structural changes in our society, much less the prison industrial complex.

In any case, Keltner contends that power makes us impulsive sociopaths. His workplace studies found that power leads to poor impulse control and inappropriate behaviours such as extreme risk-taking, irrational and/or manipulative generosity, rudeness, "inappropriate touch" and more

---

[66] Lovelace. "Foretelling the Future."

direct flirtation (some of which I would describe as sexual harassment). People in positions of power are more likely to interrupt others, speak out of turn and fail to look at other speakers. Other nasty behavours include a higher incidence of hostility and rudeness as well as a willingness to ridicule or humiliate others. In fact, Keltner argues, powerful people often behave like patients who have damaged the orbitofrontal lobes of their brain, which plays a critical role in socially appropriate and empathetic behaviour.

The compassion circuit of the brain is correspondingly impacted by power. The less empathy one feels, the less inclined one is to take action to alleviate another's suffering. Power disengages compassion.[67]

It's important, however, not to generalize about folks who lack empathetic response. For example, people with autism and posttraumatic stress disorder have empathy failures for reasons other than enjoying power.

Also, we can't forget the relational aspect of power, meaning that the social environment can impact our ability to empathize as many have observed of the rise of Nazism in Germany. The notorious Stanley Milgram experiments conducted in the 1960's are another case in point. In the first 1962 trial, students were paid to shock other students in what they believed to be a memory enhancement project. The students being shocked were actually actors called "learners" and they weren't being subjected to electrical shocks at all but faking their reactions. The students doing the shocking were called "teachers." With each wrong answer from a learner, teachers were instructed to increase the electrical charge with which they "shocked" the subject. Learners, who could be heard but not seen by teachers, screamed in supposed pain, begged for mercy and went silent to simulate losing consciousness. Sixty-three percent of the "teachers" in this experiment, urged on by the scientist overseeing the study, the authority figure in the room, took the experiment all the way to its bitter end when the learner faked losing consciousness. Many of the 63% questioned the scientist's direction to continue with the shocks but they still carried out those directives.

In subsequent experiments that included women as "teachers" and "learners," fewer teachers were willing to administer shocks all the way to the passing out stage. Seeing the learners' supposed suffering, rather than only hearing it, also discouraged teachers from continuing with shocks. In addition, when actors planted in the lab spoke against scientists who urged increasingly painful shocks, this also resulted in less cooperation among "teachers." Orders to continue the shocks when issued by non-scientists similarly decreased "teacher" compliance.

---

[67] Dr. Keltner, Dacher. "The Power Paradox". Greater Good Science Centre. Winder 2007-08. http://greatergood.berkeley.edu/article/item/power_paradox/

When the Milgram experiments are discussed in popular culture, it's usually the initial one that is cited. Information from the subsequent experiments in which much less than half the participants were willing to administer the most painful of shocks, suggests that the social environment impacted decisions to disobey the scientist's directives. So, social standards, norms and values definitely have a role to play. As an activist I find it particularly interesting that when an actor spoke against the scientist's directives it influenced the teachers to defy those directives. This demonstrates the crucial role that activists can play in advising people not to comply with wrongdoing and arguing against the logics that attempt to rationalize injustice. Nevertheless, in every Milgram experiment there were some people who willingly administered seemingly painful shocks to volunteers in what was understood to be nothing more than a memory experiment.

Scientists of the day were trying to understand what made humans cruel. Despite the infamous "only following orders" claims of Nazi's who were tried as war criminals in the late 1940's, the "following orders" rationalization did not hold up among the "teachers" in this series of experiments.

What motivated teachers to shock learners to the point of unconsciousness was even more chilling. In their post experiment interviews, teachers explained that they were trying to be cooperative volunteers who supported the overall objectives of the research project. While they may have experienced qualms, the teachers didn't feel coerced to administer shocks. They thought they were serving the interests of an experiment being carried out to benefit humanity.

So, the question lingers: how much pain can we be convinced to inflict on others in the interest of some "greater good" concept? Are we social justice advocates equally vulnerable to harming others because we are convinced that the ultimate goal of our actions is beneficial to humanity over the long term? As activists we engage in many discussions about tactics and strategies. I often wonder how the capacity to empathize impacts such conversations and the actions that follow.

In the discussion about what prohibits empathetic reactions, some scientists say that you are more likely to empathize with people like you: in your family, class, racial group, and so on. However, there are clearly many who are capable of empathizing with people who are unlike them. And, as in the first Milgram experiment, where learners, teachers and scientists were all white, middle class and male, it is clear that people from similar social locations can lack empathy for each other. In those days the scanning equipment we have now wasn't available so we have no idea if the teachers felt empathy for the learners they shocked into unconsciousness. We can only speculate about how they found a way to quell their intrinsic empathic and compassionate responses.

Now we more clearly understand that our early childhood and even adult experiences of emotional connection and trauma have a stronger impact on our capacity to empathize because they impact the development of neural pathways in the brain. As mentioned previously, children who suffer or witness domestic violence, for example, are more likely to behave violently as adults, demonstrating a failed capacity to empathize. Their empathy circuit was broken in childhood.

More recently, compassion experts have learned that it's much more difficult to call up compassion when you don't feel safe. You're much more likely to access compassion if you're living in a safe environment and/or if your childhood was characterized by safety and security. That doesn't mean that people don't manage it anyway – or act as if they do, faking it until they feel it. I also wonder how much one's *perception* of safety and security impact their capacity to muster compassion.

I recall as a university student in the 1980's sitting in on testimony to a Human Rights Tribunal investigating the then-current Civil War in El Salvador. The first testimony I heard was from a woman who told of being kidnapped as a teenager by the military after her family had been massacred and her village burnt to the ground. She described being held for days, chained to a pole on the grounds of the military base, raped and beaten several times a day by soldiers until one of them finally helped her escape into the night. After hearing that story I wondered how people such as these soldiers could be so cruel and without conscience. My answer arrived with the next witness.

This testimony came from an ex-soldier, a deserter from the Salvadoran army. This man, then in his mid twenties, described how as a twelve year old he had watched the military kill the men in his family, rape and murder his mother and sisters, then force him to join them. He and other young boys his age endured weeks of beatings and were force-fed mystery drugs that made them feel strong, fast and generally powerful. After this treatment, the man said, he was taken out to face some prisoners from another village. A gun was placed in his hand. Another was pointed at his head. He was told to murder the villagers. He pulled the trigger. After that no one needed to force him to do drugs. The boy became a man and finally decided to desert, fleeing north to Mexico and eventually to Canada.

Stories such as these emerge out of many conflicts, historically and currently. Yet, clearly we have known for a very long time that torturers and otherwise brutal and cruel people are molded, fashioned and constructed, purposefully or neglectfully, by their social environment. As activists, we know this and can offer a gazillion stories, studies and statistics to demonstrate it. Until now, however, we've relied on social, "soft" science data. Now we have hard science to back us up.

The social "soft" science tells us that child bullies are at higher risk of depression, suicide attempts, drug abuse, violent crimes as well as being neglectful and abusive parents. Low empathy also corresponds with feeling less physical pain. Hard science shows us that bullies are incapable of "mirroring" another's pain. Mirroring is something your healthy brain does when you see another suffering. For example, if you see a child fall off a swing in the playground, your brain reacts in exactly the same way as the child in pain. The only difference is that there is an additional part of your brain that tells you "that child is not you" and with that information you are able to respond to the child's suffering appropriately.

Not so with bully brains. Unlike the brains of autistic children, which are incapable of recognizing suffering and pain because that part of their brains doesn't function properly, the bully brain recognizes another's pain but other parts of the empathy circuit are broken. So they don't "mirror" and they don't feel the need to act to relieve another's suffering. In fact, they get a reaction in their brain's pleasure centre.

Social science has suggested that there are basically two reactions to trauma: one being hyper-sensitivity and the other being a lack of sensitivity to the pain and suffering of others. The bully brains of White supremacists, homophobes and just plain old mean people are broken (though not irreparably) and chances are it's because their life experiences wired their brains in such a way that they have difficulty accessing compassion. Not surprising since unhealthy and dysfunctional societies produce unhealthy and dysfunctional people.

Whatever the cause, we two-leggeds can obviously be empathetic, apathetic or bullies. Choice is only one of many influences on whether we experience compassion or not. As we've already seen, our choices are impacted by our physical and social environments -- historical and current. I would suggest that a dominant worldview that emphasizes our inter-relatedness might be more conducive to influencing people with empathy failure to choose empathy, even when they don't necessarily feel it. A common knowledge of the risks and disadvantages of bullying versus the benefits derived from empathy and compassion might be persuasive. Who doesn't want to feel happier and be healthier, after all? Individual choices to behave in empathetic and compassionate ways will not only be socially reinforced, they will increasingly re-shape the brain to facilitate more of the same and generate their own rewards. Education that teaches us how we can personally benefit, particularly health wise, from sharing with and caring about others might motivate everything from better parenting practices to more a equitable distribution of social wealth.

Catching compassion

Most people recognize that we two-leggeds are inherently social creatures, seeking each other out and working together with varying amounts of success to get our physical and emotional needs met. Certainly in the relational worldview the relatively recent understanding of *biophilia*, the tendency of life to seek and affiliate with life, was foundational. As we saw earlier, our very understanding of who we are and how we function in the world depends on our relationships. If our relationships are caring and compassionate we benefit. That is scientific fact. A more surprising fact is that *observers* of kindness and compassion also benefit. In exploring this, please allow me a small digression.

I've just returned from a workshop at the 2012 Toronto Anarchist Bookfair, something I never envisioned doing even a year ago because I had convinced myself that I didn't agree with anarchism. Having had some virtual and face-to-face conversations with anarchists, I realize that anarchy and Indigenism may have some points of intersection. Besides, even though I don't identify as an anarchist I figure, since many of my readers identify as such and I offer friendly critiques of anarchist theories and activities in my writings, I have an obligation to stay current on anarchist thinking. I attended parts of this conference, first of all, to learn about the activities of the "Anti-Authoritarian Indigenous/People of Colour Caucus" (which I won't discuss here) and secondly, to participate in a workshop titled "Anarchist Visions of Life After Capitalism."

Before I continue let me clarify that I use the word capitalism in the same way that Marx did, to describe an economic system where a minority of people in society own and control the means of production for the purposes of making a profit while others sell their labour or otherwise function outside of that power relationship in order to survive. I understand there are other definitions out there and I don't mean to impose my own but I do want to be clear on what *I* mean by "capitalism."

In any case, the presentation at the anarchist conference provided an outline of two models of possible post-capitalist economic structures for comparison and discussion: 1) Economic Democracy as described by David Schweickart and 2) Participatory Economics (Parecon) as framed by Michael Albert and Robin Hahnel. There were many questions and critiques of both models offered by participants and, unfortunately not enough time for thorough discussion (when is there ever?), but it was noted that the potential effectiveness of the Parecon model seemed to depend a great deal on the inherent altruistic tendencies, generosity and cooperation of the human spirit.

I can't possibly do justice to summarizing the Parecon model here but a foundational idea in this framework has workplaces organizing into workers' councils and predicting how much they would like to produce in a year. Likewise, consumers, organized into household and neighbourhood councils, predict how much they would like to consume in a year. "Like," "want," and "need" are key words because the idea is that to enjoy a quality of life, workers may not want to spend 40 hours of their week producing clothing, electronics or even food for others but may only want to spend 15 hours doing that. In addition, consumers may not initially limit their "wants" to subsistence goods and might desire luxury items that put pressure on producers (not to mention resources).

In any case, the model proposes a centralized body, the Iteration Facilitation Board (IFB), which would compile data from both sets of councils, analyze discrepancies and disparities between consumption and production and thereafter facilitate negotiations toward consensus among groups of producers and consumers in the interest of balancing supply and demand. Now, I'm sure, particularly in light of my sketchy description, you can find much to critique and question in this model. The issue of sustainability came to my mind. What is the relationship of two-leggeds to land and resources in this model? Where is there an analysis of how much the land and Our Relations will bear in terms of meeting human wants and needs? What happens when the exploitation of resources to satisfy the wants or possibly even the needs of one community jeopardizes the wellbeing of another?

The presenter in this session responded to this critique by stating that the principle of decision-making proposed in Parecon gives people who are most affected by a decision the most say in it. However, he admitted the model as presented lacked details around this particular question. His response also doesn't take into consideration the concern for sustainability as my Indigenous teachings conceptualize it, that is, the long-term ability of life to regenerate itself – all life, not just the human form.

However, I digress (again) and to be fair to the model you should probably have a read yourself of what Albert and Hahnel are specifically proposing. Despite my critique, I appreciate its optimism, among other things, which segues nicely into one issue I'd like to focus on here: the proposition that human beings would be motivated to work to produce consumer items and services simply out of concern for the "wants" of others. The model also posits that consumers will willingly adjust their demands to accommodate the desires and needs of producers.

Many self-described anarchists at the presentation expressed doubts that human beings are inherently that generous and caring of each other, not to mention honest. I would have done the same if I'd attended that workshop prior to doing my research for this book. But some surprising findings of economists and scientists suggest I would be wrong.

Economist Daniel H. Pink has both conducted and cited many studies from the likes of the London School of Economics and other pro-business institutions that indicate that, once their survival needs are satisfied and people are assured of comfortable living conditions, they are cooperative, generous and quite motivated to share in meaningful ways. He notes, for example, that people who work 40+ hours a week in the software development industry go home and spend their free time developing open source applications, some of which you've probably downloaded onto your computer or phone.

Another example Pink talks about in his work is that of Red Gate Software, a firm based in Cambridge that makes development tools for programmers. Initially Red Gate's compensation to its sales staff was commission-based and they did not receive any salary. This provided a competitive environment where the motivation for sales was to make the maximum amount of commission. Sales managers spent more time policing and justifying compensation as well managing conflicts among sales staff than they did on any other work. When Red Gate began to offer its employees a healthy flat salary, the sales staff began to act more like a team. They supported and encouraged each other, even shared leads and information. The focus moved from selling for the highest dollar to providing high quality products and service; from maximizing commission to maximizing customer satisfaction. The time of managers was freed up to work on other tasks.

Pink's work provides examples and studies, conducted in many parts of the world, wealthy and poor societies alike, which demonstrate that, once people's subsistence and sustainability needs are met, they can become more productive, cooperative and generous as well as creative. There is one qualification that Pink makes regarding these findings and that is that this is only the case for work that requires creative, strategic and critical thinking skills – which is probably the majority of the jobs available in North America these days. His findings don't hold up when it comes to work that is routine, mundane and doesn't require a lot of critical thinking.

Another caution for activists is that Pink is really all about finding ways of supporting the business sector by enhancing employee productivity and generating larger profits for corporations. It may not be what ultimately motivates him but his work is tailored for use in the corporate sector. For example, he discusses one software developer that gives its employees one day per month to work on whatever they choose. So they spend every other day doing their jobs but on this particular day of the month they get to indulge their desires, imagination and creativity. The company does this because it benefits the bottom line. Apparently, a large percentage of upgrades and new products the business offers every year are conceptualized and developed on these days.

Nevertheless, Pink's work might be useful in terms of better understanding what motivates cooperation and generosity, as well as how cooperation impacts relationships among individuals, communities and Our

Relations; how cooperation enhances the quality of life while at the same time enhancing human productivity. Indeed, there is no shortage of examples, studies and theories in the literature that demonstrate that cooperation and diversity enhance creativity. Much of it comes from the pro-business, pro-capitalist sector. Clearly, despite the rhetorical idealization of competition, the reality is that capitalist institutions cooperate, collaborate and partner with each other all the time in order to maximize their profits. Setting prices, paying political lobbyists to influence lawmakers and joint marketing ventures are only some of many examples of this. Consequently, I won't review much more of the social science here. Instead, let's move on to the hard science that supports the notion that generosity and cooperation make for healthy individuals and communities.

As we've already discussed, feeling, thinking and expressing appreciation, compassion, and gratitude positively impact our individual health. Such emotions are expressed and felt in instances of cooperation. As a result, we can logically assume that cooperation positively impacts the health of those cooperating. Furthermore, acts of kindness generate benefits for the person committing the act, the recipients of the act as well as anyone witnessing it. The research talks about observers of kindnesses benefiting from a "helper's high" marked by the activation of the reward circuit in the brain as well as high levels of endorphins and serotonin in the bloodstream. Serotonin stabilizes moods, decreases anxiety and moderates the cardiovascular system. Endorphins create feelings of euphoria, enhance endurance, moderate appetite, increase libido, enhance immunity and dampen physical pain. The feel-good effects of endorphins are probably well known because of information readily available around the benefits of exercise, during which your body also releases these chemicals. As it turns out you can get some of the benefits of exercise by just being kind, caring and helpful to others. People who watch you will benefit similarly.

The term *Mother Teresa Effect* comes from Behavioural Psychologist David McClelland, who had the saliva of his Harvard students analyzed before and after they viewed a film on the work of Mother Teresa. He noted that viewing the film resulted in higher levels of an antibody. This antibody remained at heightened levels for several hours if and when he had his students recall times they had been involved in giving or receiving. Hence the conclusion of this and other studies: that witnessing kindness enhances immunity.

All of this presumes, of course, that the acts of kindness, volunteering, cooperation and so on are not done out of a sense of obligation, fear or anger; that they are not done out of routine or habit, and that they are not causing undue stress on the people undertaking these activities. Otherwise, you don't get the benefits and aren't likely to project them to witnesses either. So activists need to take note here.

Concerning the power of touch, caring, physical contact activates the vagal response, lights up the reward circuit in the brain, calms cardiovascular stress and releases oxytocin into the bloodstream in both the "toucher" and the "touchee." Studies have also shown: holding and embracing premature babies boosts their weight gain by 47%; when health care workers intentionally use caring touch on Alzheimers patients it decreases the sufferers' instance of depression; doctors who engage in sympathetic touch positively impact patient outcomes in terms of faster healing and longer survival rates.

Neuroplasticity research conducted at Stanford University concluded that when you practice "deep listening" (make eye contact, sympathetic noises, engage in particular body language) the amygdala and hippocampus of the other person starts to "cool down", (show less activity). The amygdala processes emotions like fear and anxiety. Among the functions of the hippocampus is the processing of memory. Perhaps being listened to allows you to assign less importance to the root memory triggered by what is upsetting or agitating you in the moment. (It has been noted by experts on anger that we rarely are angered exclusively by what happens in the moment. Rather, what happens in the moment triggers a reaction to something that jeopardized our sense of safety and security in the past.) Attentive listening not only changes the brain *activity* of another person but also changes the very *structure* of their brain, as we noted in "Jedi Brain Tricks." As anger, agitation and upset dissipate or "cool down," these brain changes decrease the impact of stress.

So, we are starting to see some hard science that backs up the idea that being genuinely kind, generous, and caring promotes health for givers, recipients and observers. Cultivating these emotions in our relationships and interactions creates a win/win/win scenario for all concerned.

Electro-magnetism – A Direct Energy Connection

The Institute of HeartMath is doing remarkable work studying the electro-magnetism (EM) of relationships and interactions. Electro-magnetism is produced wherever there is electrical current. Our bodies produce bio-electrical current, as we've previously discussed, particularly in the nervous system. Consequently, every cell and organ of our body produces an EM field. Your brain and heart produce the largest EM fields, but your heart's magnetic field is thousands of times stronger than that of your brain. This energy constantly radiates out from your body.

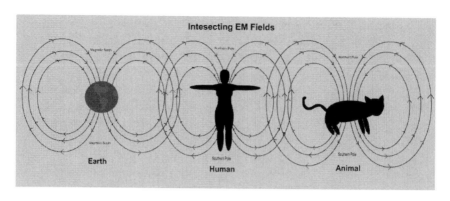

In responding to your emotions, as well as other information it gets from around your body, your heart generates bio-electrical current that communicates with your brain and other body parts. As the current changes so does the vibration of your heart's magnetic field. Consequently, emotional and other information encoded into this magnetic field also changes. Hence, your emotional state is reflected in your heart's EM field.

It is currently possible to detect the heart's EM field several feet outside the body. Amazingly, we have determined that people can impact each other's HRV patterns through their EM fields. For example, the rhythms between two people who are sitting close together can sync up, that is, harmonize to the same frequency and wavelength. This can happen between complete strangers, though the closer the emotional connection between people, as in romantic pairs, intimate friends and family members, the quicker the syncing. Furthermore, and even more amazing, one person's HRV pattern can show up in someone else's EEG (brain) scan. This is one way that can happen: Salima is happy to see Keshig. Her heart rate changes, changing her EM field. Keshig's EM field syncs up with Salima's. His EM communicates with his heart, which communicates happiness to his brain. Hence, Keshig's mood is lifted by Salima's presence. So both your brain and heart are sensitive to your emotions as well as those of other people. Feelings are indeed contagious.

Emotional contagion has been theorized by scientists who study the tendency of human beings to mimic each other's facial expressions, vocalizations and body language. The work at HeartMath, however, focuses on measuring changes in EM, HRV and EEG profiles; measuring the energetic output of our bodies and the impact of it. Anyway, not only can your heart tell *your* brain what to do, it can communicate with *someone else's* brain. My guess is the more grounded and centred you are in the information you're radiating, the more influence you're going to have over another person within range of your EM field. If your emotional response is based in something that is outside of yourself and isn't coming from your own spirit, it's easily influenced by external forces and can shift and wane with external events. But if your feelings are deeply engrained, cultivated and coming from your own self-generated disposition, it's less likely external forces are going to shake you up significantly.

This relates to theories about baseline emotional states or emotional set points. The idea is that if we are basically and intrinsically compassionate, grateful and positive we will still appropriately experience the full range of emotions in response to our environments and relationships but we will return eventually to our set point, our positive centre. This is, unfortunately, just as true if your emotional set point is one of anger, depression or fear.

Thanks to plasticity generally and neuroplasticity in particular, you can train yourself to readjust your set point to a positive place, as we've seen in previous chapters. This involves intentionally cultivating and nurturing gratitude, compassion and appreciation. The more you do this, the faster and more effectively you reset your emotional baseline/set point. (There are some limitations we'll discuss in the "Shape-shifting Tricksters" chapter.)

As an activist, how do you take responsibility for the emotions you radiate? Certainly, you are entitled to your feelings and, as we discussed, experiencing a full range of emotions makes for a healthy, fulfilling life. The question of responsibility in this context relates more to people who are stuck in negativity; whose emotional set points are depression, anger or hate. You can probably imagine, if you don't already know, the toll it takes on our spirit to deal with a loved one who is depressed. If you're the one mired in depression, anger or some other negative emotion, what are your responsibilities to your loved ones? Do you feel a responsibility to shift your temperament so you can radiate emotional health? It would seem to me that taking responsibility for our emotional wellbeing is a prerequisite to any claim on being a social justice activist.

There are volumes of studies emerging every day validating the energetic connections that exist between us two-leggeds. This includes discoveries about the interaction of pheromones, our bio-chemistry and our emotional responses. The upshot is we are far more connected than a materialist worldview would ever allow us to comprehend and science is only at the tip of the iceberg in terms of uncovering all the energetic ways in which we interact with each other as well as the other life forms on the planet and beyond. And on that note let's take a look at our relationships with the rest of Our Relations.

Energetic Connections Across Species

Technology has found ways of making it rain under the right conditions by seeding clouds with chemicals, some of which are suspected of causing harm to the environment and human health. This is done routinely at airports, for example. So we humans are quite capable of making it rain. But do you believe that under the right conditions, with the right protocols and the right group doing the right thing at the right time, people can make rain through ceremony?

I won't be surprised if you're skeptical but maybe by the end of this chapter you'll have eliminated at least some of those doubts.

To start, let me tell you about a science experiment my youngest son conducted at the age of about nine or ten for a school assignment. He had me buy him two coriander seedlings in pots. The seedlings were about the same size, length and breadth. The plants were treated in exactly the same way in terms of their physical care: sitting side by side on our patio they got the same amount of sunshine and water every day. The only difference? My son took one the two seedlings, gave it a name and daily took it into his room for about half an hour. In this half hour he would talk to it, read to it, play music for it, and generally pay it positive attention. Then, when the time was up, he would return the plant to its place beside the other.

I'm sure you can guess how the story ends. The seedling that received all the attention outgrew its partner. By the end of four weeks, it was both longer and fuller by about 1/4, as my son determined with a measuring tape as well as his naked eye. Of course, on its own that experiment proves nothing - but it does reflect the experience of many people who develop relationships with their plants. This story demonstrates a way of thinking that is common to relational worldviews, which hold that if you actively appreciate the beauty and bounty of Mother Earth, She will enrich and expand on what She has given you. But if you're still stuck in the dominant worldview you may want to consider the why, if we, as human beings, can impact each other through our EM fields, can't we similarly impact plants and animals? And they us?

Take pets for example. You have only to Google the subject and you'll find tons of information on the benefits of owning a pet. Pets lower your blood pressure, lessen your anxiety and boost your immunity. Assuming you're not afraid, merely petting a cat or dog slows the heart rate, counters the stress reaction, and elevates dopamine and serotonin levels while lowering triglyceride and cholesterol ("bad" fat) levels. Pet owners are less likely to suffer from depression and are more likely to recover from or live longer after serious events like stroke and heart attack. People who own pets make less frequent doctor and hospital visits and enjoy better overall health. Studies show that Alzheimer's patients have fewer outbursts when there is a pet in the household.[68] Men with AIDS are less likely to

---

[68] http://www.dummies.com/how-to/content/calming-alzheimers-patients-with-pet-visitations.html

suffer from depression if they own a pet.[69] Perhaps more surprising is that, contrary to previous beliefs, children raised in homes where there are pets are at less risk of allergies, asthma and eczema.[70]

You may assume these better health statistics are due to the slightly increased physical exercise that pet owners get and you'd be partly right. You do have to clean litter boxes, walk dogs and carry home pet food. But it's also true that laughing at your pet, and caring for and about an animal, calls up emotions like appreciation, gratitude and joy, and we know such feelings generate the best states of health.

Going deeper into the question, we can return to the work of HeartMath, which has demonstrated how the HRV between a young boy and his dog, when in range of each other's EM fields, can and do sync up. This indicates emotional syncing across species. I'll let you do the heartmath on that data but clearly we humans have the capacity to impact animals and they us, though there's still much to be learned.

Our relationship to the Earth Herself is essential to our wellbeing. As we discussed earlier, Indigenous and other peoples consider the Earth a living, sentient being, as much as the life that generates on and within Her. We are equally connected to Father Sun, without whom life on this planet could not exist. This excerpted oral teaching I've paraphrased below demonstrates this and other values of First Nations peoples such as gender balance, roles, and responsibilities.

> *Father Sun rises every day, whether we see him or not. He doesn't beat or stomp his way into the world. Rather he baths us all in his warmth and light. He and Mother Earth provide us with all that we two-leggeds need to live and grow.*

Indigenous societies and others have recognized for millennia that we humans have more than a physical dependence on the Earth and Our Relations. We have an energetic dependence as well. Science finds a basis for this relationship in such forms of energy as electro-magnetism, gravitational forces and the Sun's radiation that penetrates the Earth's atmosphere. In fact, our relationship to the Earth and the Sun means that the sicker Our Relations become as a result of human foolishness in

---

[69] Robak, Warren. "UCLA Researchers Find That AIDS Patients Who Own Pets are Less Likely to Suffer From Depression", UCLA News. May 1999. http://newsroom.ucla.edu/portal/ucla/PRN-UCLA-Researchers-Find-That-AIDS-36.aspx

[70] Davis, Jeanie Lerche. "5 Ways Pets Can Improve Your Health" WebMD Feature. Reviewed by Brunilda Nazario, MD. **http://www.webmd.com/hypertension-high-blood-pressure/guide/5-ways-pets-improve-your-health**

pouring toxins into our environment or depleting the Earth of essential resources, the sicker we become mentally and emotionally as well as physically (particularly in recognition that there isn't a clear delineation between the mental, emotional and physical self or the internal and external environment).

As a speculative fiction nerd, I've often parted company with segments of fandom, writers and filmmakers that depict futures where humans are sealed off from our messy natural environment as if it is desirable. In the *Star Trek* universe, humans of the 23rd and 24th centuries live out their entire lives in starships and space stations, never needing a connection to sunshine, soil or the natural world. In the short-lived *Firefly* series, the character of Zoe declares in one episode how much she hates the noise and disorder of planets and waxes nostalgic about the hum of metal under her feet. Not to generalize about speculative fiction, because there is plenty of it that celebrates the connection of humans (or aliens) to the natural environment, the notion of utopia as a world where nature is controlled, separate and irrelevant to human existence is a familiar trope. The idea is that so long as the natural world, somewhere else, provides for our food, clothing and other physical and material needs, we can survive quite nicely. With starship hulls or space station walls between us and the natural environment, humans can lead an ideal existence without having to deal with weather, animals or anything messy and unpredictable. In these stories, the most important relationships tend to be among humans or between humans and technology. Even so, some brilliant observations and critiques of human societies and the human condition are made. But utopian? Desirable? Not in my opinion. Not in terms of how human organisms are built.

A very simple way to begin to understand your energetic connection to the Earth and the Sun is by looking at Vitamin D, which is produced by our skin on exposure to direct sunlight, specifically, ultra-violet radiation (UV energy). It's virtually impossible to get all the Vitamin D your body needs through diet and supplements. Diseases that can occur due to vitamin D deficiency include osteoporosis, various types of cancer and rickets. A deficiency of vitamin D has implications for other illnesses and conditions too, exacerbating their harmful impact. You can also become clinically depressed as a result of vitamin D deficiency, if you do not get enough exposure to the Sun's UV energy. How this gets looked after for the crews of *Deep Space Nine* or the *USS Enterprise*, I have no idea.

Looking at circadian rhythms is another way of understanding our energetic connections to the Earth and Sun. The simple rhythms of night and day have significant influence on your body. Sunset impacts the pineal gland behind your eyes, which communicates with the Suprachiasmatic nucleus (a part of our brain that regulates a minimum of ten bio-rhythms).

Darkness signals a series of reactions that basically tell your body to produce melatonin, which makes you sleepy. Once asleep you go through sleep cycles where your body engages in different activities that are essential to your wellbeing. These include tissue repair, boosting the immune system, detoxification and so on.

If you are not exposed to cycles of light and dark, such as one scientist who spent a month sealed in a cave exploring his biorhythms, your circadian rhythm defaults to whatever your genes mandate. You might experience sleep/wake patterns that are based in 25-28 hour cycles, roughly spending 1/3 of that time in sleep. But when you are exposed to the light and dark of sunrise and sunset, that diurnal rhythm overrides your genetic predisposition and your sleep cycle settles into the 24-hour pattern.

Of course, today we have artificial lighting, which takes us out of sync with Earth rhythms. Shift work, stimulants and sedatives don't do much for our biological clocks either. Add the impact of stress to that and it's a wonder that anyone gets enough sleep these days. In fact, experts claim most people in North America are sleep deprived. As I write this I've just returned from what should have been a meeting with a fellow activist. He texted to apologize, telling me he is "clinically exhausted" and his doctor has ordered him to rest and catch up on his sleep for the next ten days. Personally, I'm surprised more activists don't suffer from chronic fatigue, adrenal exhaustion or any other number of ailments resulting from stress-filled lifestyles.

The importance of adequate sleep at nighttime is being increasingly understood as a crucial contributor to physical wellbeing. There is a lot of emerging science on the topic of sleep and sleep cycles that I don't want to examine in great detail here. I simply want to note that we are impacted by the night/day and seasonal rhythms of the planet we live on, including the sun that shines down on it, and this is another example of our energetic connection to natural cycles and patterns. Like it or not, we are tied to the Earth and Her cosmic relations and attempting to alter or control those rhythms or our responses to them can be harmful to our wellbeing.

I've just finished reading an article, for example, on how silver iodide lessened the expected severity of a hailstorm that was predicted to hit Calgary, Alberta yesterday. As I interact with staff at the Indigenous Environmental Network on Facebook I note that insurance companies are quite pleased with themselves for averting an estimated $20 million in property damage. Who knows how much they spent on enlisting six airplanes to fly for 26 hours seeding clouds? Who knows what health and environmental issues could result? The future health care and environmental costs of burning the necessary fuel and spraying out silver iodide were not tabulated in the news reports.

More and more information is coming to light about how humans react to the noises and smells of our environment. The sounds of chirping birds and babbling brooks as well as the smell of lavender all have a calming effect on our biochemistry, as producers of relaxation audio programs and aroma therapists have long understood. Howling wolves, growling bears and the smell of decay have the opposite effect. The reasons are obvious. Chirping birds signify that no predators are about and we can relax. Babbling brooks hold the promise of quenching our thirst and/or cooling ourselves on a hot day. Growls and howls signify potential danger nearby and we need to be alert. Unpleasant smells discourage us from consuming what we otherwise might consider a source of sustenance while pleasant smells relax us and signal that nourishment or something equally pleasant (like spring) is at hand. The pleasant smell of lavender may encourage people to pick it or be around it, thus allowing them to benefit form its insect repellant properties. Studies have shown that men find lavender sexually arousing so it might be one of many of Mother Earth's ways of encouraging us two-leggeds to bond romantically and reproduce. These are just some of various ways that we can begin to understand how we connect to the Earth in energetic ways. There are many benefits that we receive as a result of spending time in nature but what happens when we fail to interact regularly with Our Relations?

Psychiatrist Richard Louv has coined the term *Nature Deficit Disorder* to characterize mental and emotional illness that results from modern lifestyles that isolate us from the rest of the natural world. He defines Nature Deficit Disorder (NDD) as "an atrophied awareness, a diminished ability to find meaning in the life that surrounds us."[71] Louv's work focuses on the mind/body/nature connection.

A case can easily be made for the physical disadvantages of leading sedentary, indoor lifestyles. All the research on the benefits of physical activity clearly shows that our overall health suffers if we don't get enough exercise, sunshine and fresh air. A recently discovered bacterium, *Mycobacterium vaccae*, found in soil and often breathed in or ingested when we come into contact with nature, is being researched for the role it may have as an anti-depressant. This microorganism stimulates serotonin and norepinephrine in the brain as well as neurogenesis (development of brain cells). Scientists believe this bacteria enhances learning because of serotonin's role in improving memory. [72] Furthermore, for better or worse, m*ycobacterium vaccae* is currently being researched for its potential to create vaccines for some types of asthma as well as cancer, Crohn's disease,

---

[71] Reference here.
[72] "Can Bacteria Make You Smarter?", Science Daly, May 24, 2010.
http://www.sciencedaily.com/releases/2010/05/100524143416.htm

depression, leprosy, psoriasis, dermatitis, eczema, rheumatoid arthritis and tuberculosis.[73] Oncologist Mary O'Brien of the Royal Marsden Hospital in London inoculated lung cancer patients with a strain of *M. vaccae* and found that that patients experienced improved emotional health, vitality and even cognitive function while their cancer symptoms decreased.[74]

An Indigenous response to this might suggest that just spending more time in nature might satisfy the role scientists look toward vaccines to play. Increasingly, scientists operating out of the mainstream paradigm are coming to understand how much nature prevents some illness and provides antidotes to diseases that impact modern society. For example, senior assistant professor of forest medicine at Nippon Medical School in Tokyo, Li Qing has theorized that the breathing in of antimicrobial essential wood oils given off by plants (phytoncides) might explain one reason why contact with the natural world enhances our immune system.[75] Louv further points to a study that links nearsightedness with increased time spent indoors under artificial lights looking at TV and computer screens. These studies illustrate the material/physical connection we human beings have to "nature". They show the many ways exchanging bio-chemicals or micro-organisms with "nature" can support our wellbeing. This contrasts with practices in mainstream society that suggest an underlying fear of nature and the perceived need for humans to be protected from or in control of the environment.

None of this is meant to suggest that the natural world does not pose some threat to human health and safety. There are diseases, predators and natural disasters that also reside in our environments. Also, there are dangers to our health that have been exacerbated due to human intervention in natural cycles, rhythms and patterns. Genetically altering crops to be inherent insecticides, for example, has contributed to the world's dangerously decreasing population of honeybees. Because honeybees are responsible for so much pollination their decreasing numbers are having an impact on the plant world which in turn impacts the animal world, including us two-leggeds. The point I'm making is that our health and safety is hardly guaranteed by isolating ourselves from or attempting to control nature and that, in fact, interacting closely with the environment, despite potential risks, is crucial to our quality of life and even

[73] According to Wikipedia as well as ibid.

[74] Sachs, Naomi. "Dirt Can Make You Happy", *Horticulture: The Art & Science of Smart Gardening.* January 25, 2011. http://www.hortmag.com/blogs/gardening-blog/dirt-can-make-you-happy

[75] Louv, Richard. "The Nature Principle: Reconnecting with Life in a Virtual Age", *The Nature Principal.* Algonquin Books of Chapel Hill, © 2011, 2012 http://noetic.org/noetic/issue-twenty-three-june/the-nature-principle/

our very survival. Furthermore, mainstream science is only now becoming aware of the many energetic and spiritual ways in which life impacts life.

It's important to note that scientists continue to debate what *nature* means. Some discourse suggests that if we consider humans a part of the "natural" world, all that we create can be considered *nature*, including city buildings, plastics and technological wonders, to name a few. Even if we consider "nature" and what is "natural" to be defined in relation the degree to which humans have influenced or interfered with it, we would have still a hard time understanding what constituted the "natural world" in materialist/mainstream scientific terms. Yet, however we want to define *nature*, emerging studies provide some intriguing information about how our energetic connections to Our Relations (or what Indigenous peoples consider non-human life forms) impact our wellbeing. The concept of "nature therapy" is gaining increased credibility in conventional medical circles. Prescriptions that involve intimate, longer and more frequent connections to nature have been helpful in moderating pain and alleviating negative stress reactions, as well as for improving the conditions of people with heart disease, dementia, and other health issues.[76]

Louv cites a number of studies on this topic. One compares the rate of recovery for patients in a Pennsylvania hospital and found that those with windows looking out on a landscape full of deciduous trees spent an average of 24 hours less in hospital than their counterparts whose windows faced a brick wall. Patients who had access to the view of trees also required, on average, less pain medication. Another study found that the artificially produced sounds of nature and access to a mural of an outdoor landscape impacted how well sedated patients undergoing bronchoscopy managed their pain. Compared to their counterparts, who only received sedation and did not get the nature therapy, the group exposed to *fake* nature had better capacity to control their pain.[77]

Yet another study compared the body mass index (BMI) of children in neighbourhoods with and without "green spaces" and found that those who had access to green spaces had lower BMI's.[78] Similar research shows that kids who play in nature, rather than in concrete playgrounds, demonstrate increased attentiveness in school, improved test scores, better understanding of science concepts, enhanced self esteem, improved behavior, enhanced creativity, improved memory and better overall health

---

[76] Louv, Richard. "The Nature Principle: Reconnecting with Life in a Virtual Age", *The Nature Principal.* Algonquin Books of Chapel Hill, © 2011, 2012 http://noetic.org/noetic/issue-twenty-three-june/the-nature-principle/

[77] Ibid.
[78] Ibid.

as well as better problem solving, critical thinking and decision-making skills.[79] Louv posits that ADHD (Attention Deficit Hyperactivity Disorder), an increasingly common diagnosis being applied to young boys, as well as other physical health issues are directly related to our indoor, sedentary, nature-deprived lifestyle.

North American scientists aren't the only ones gaining insights into the issue. Japanese researchers have found that people who merely gaze at forest scenery have lower levels of cortisol in their saliva. As a result of this and other research, "forest medicine" or "forest bathing" is an increasingly credible approach to the treatment of a variety of health issues in Japan. Studies at Nippon Medical School in Tokyo have determined that, after controlling for many influencing factors, exercising in nature as opposed to being indoors and/or in outdoor urban areas brought about an added advantage of heightened immunity and a stronger anti-stress reaction.[80]

There are a variety of theories as to why contact with nature, even imagined, has such a powerful positive impact on our physical, mental and emotional wellbeing. But this knowledge has been understood and utilized by First Nations people for centuries in healing and other forms of ceremonies. Simply being in the presence of plants and animals, being "on the land," is understood in Indigenous cultures to be automatically and intrinsically healing. From a relational point of view, energetic interactions with nature evoke a sense of connection, awe and gratitude, provided the environment we are in is safe. As we've seen, such emotions generate many healthful processes in our bodies.

When you consider the rushed, stressed and urban-centred lives in which many impoverished folks live, the negative health statistics among low income and racialized communities in North America are not surprising. As activists we may want to add "access to nature" to the list of inherent, irrevocable and legally mandated human rights. Urban green spaces should take on a new significance in urban planning. Or maybe as a society we should consider whether cities make any kind of sense at all when it comes to our collective wellbeing.

Where can one draw the line between health benefits that result from physical versus energetic interactions with nature? Clearly we have essential energetic connections where even thinking about, smelling or hearing sounds associated with nature evoke positive emotions that correspond with healthful physiological responses. Is there a line to be drawn between physical and energetic interactions with nature if human beings and the

---

[79] Reference here
[80] Louv, Richard. "The Nature Principle: Reconnecting with Life in a Virtual Age", *The Nature Principal.* Algonquin Books of Chapel Hill, © 2011, 2012 http://noetic.org/noetic/issue-twenty-three-june/the-nature-principle/.

matter that comprises us and our world is mostly (or all) energy? Just as we saw when we looked at right and left brain paradigms and brain integration, perhaps there is no way one can separate the physical and the energetic.

Our Relationship with Water

In terms of our energetic relationship to life forms in nature, I am particularly interested in the results of some findings publicized by Dr. Masaru Emoto, a Japanese author and social scientist, whose work is readily accessible online. Dr. Emoto has accidentally made some potentially groundbreaking discoveries about how our mere intentions can impact the physical properties of water. Emoto took samples of polluted and clean water from around the world, froze them and then, with a dark field microscope, photographed the crystals that formed. Clean, healthy water produced geometrical, highly organized crystals. Polluted water produced poorly formed crystals or none at all. However, Dr. Emoto began to notice a relationship between different types of music he played in his lab and how healthy water crystallized. Clean water exposed to heavy metal music behaved much like polluted water when frozen. Yet clean water from the same source, when exposed to Japanese folk music, produced symmetrical crystals. Furthermore, polluted water samples, all from the same source, that did not crystallize under normal circumstances, did so after being blessed by a Buddhist monk.

With further investigation, Emoto demonstrated that water crystallization can be impacted by thoughts and feelings as well as spoken and unspoken words. His experiments had people holding water from the same source, one group thinking negative thoughts the other thinking positive ones. Water exposed to negative thinking such as "You make me sick", " I'm going to kill you." "I hate you" and "anger" did not crystallize or only partially crystallized. Words and thoughts transmitting messages such as "love," "thank you" and "peace" resulted in beautiful crystallization. Even written words simply taped onto containers of water produced the same results.

In the illustration below you'll see an artistic reproduction of photographs Emoto has published in his books and on his website.

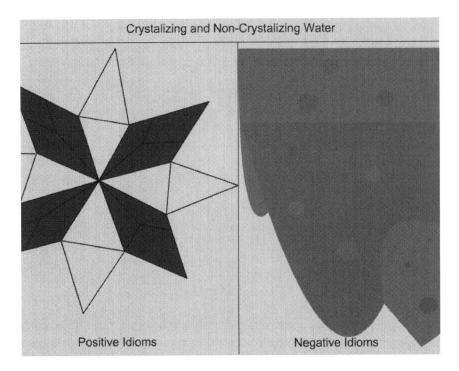

In 2008 Emoto co-authored a paper with a group of scientists at the Institute of Noetic Sciences (IONS), including Dean Radin, a Senior Scientist at IONS and Adjunct Faculty at the Department of Psychology at Sonoma State University. [81] The paper describes a study were various groups of people, under differing conditions, who focused their intentions on specific bodies of water miles away, were able to impact water crystallization patterns. Radin and Emoto co-authored an earlier peer-reviewed article in a 2006 issue of *Explore: the Journal of Science and Healing* about a different study that was also consistent with Emoto's claims.

Emoto's work has been highly criticized online and much, if not most of it, comes from anonymous sources. For those who are interested in following the debate, Dean Radin has responded to some of this criticism in his blog. [82]

From an Indigenous perspective, however, Emoto's findings are completely consistent with our understandings of how humans interact with water. When she quotes a statement put out by Elders at a gathering on her

---

[81] **Radin, D. I.**, Lund, N., Emoto, M. & Kizu, T. (2009). Triple-blind replication of the effects of distant intention on water crystal formation. *Journal of Scientific Exploration*

[82] http://noetic.org/blog/wikipedia-reader-beware-when-it-comes-psi-research/

territory, scholar, activist and former co-Chief of the Ardoch Algonquin First Nation Paula Sherman illustrates this.

> The Elders stated that *sah-kemah-wapyoe*, which translates as 'spiritual water', refers to the living water. In the spiritual sense, water is an entity that can be damaged by humans who are manipulators. We can make things happen, we can move things, we can throw things and we can break things. They characterized water as more passive, in that it will accept things done to its essence. Water will accept these changes and will undergo the same changes. It will mirror the climate or mood that we, as human beings, are in. It becomes the quality in which we shape it. We humans, in turn, are affected by the changing quality of water, and say that water is 'hurting us'. It is only giving us what we have asked of it.[83]

In my experience with First Nations as well as other Indigenous cultures, we take for granted that our intent impacts outcomes in most of our life circumstances. It's not the only factor, of course, but it has a role to play. We have many prayers and activities in our communities aimed at cleansing and raising awareness about water. In the Full Moon Ceremony, a women-only ritual, we make a "medicine" called Moon Water, which we use to help heal ourselves, family members and friends suffering physically, emotionally, mentally or spiritually. The process by which we do this is similar to the following exercise. You might want to try in your groups, collectives and communities. Start with a small group of no more than six people because the process can be time consuming.

1. All participants should bring a container of water.
2. Sit in a circle with your water.
3. Everyone in the circle names three things they're grateful for. Be sincere and dig deep.
4. Everyone in the circle takes their turn in acknowledging and thanking everyone else in the circle for some contribution they have made to the group. Again, be sincere.
5. For one minute, at the same time, everyone in the circle holds the container of water in their hands and feels grateful for it and all that it does for life.

---

[83] Dr. Sherman, Paula. "Dishonour of the Crown". Arbeiter Ring Publishing. 2008. p. 43

6. Everyone passes the container of water to the person on their right and repeats the process of holding the container of water and feeling grateful.
7. After every minute, everyone passes the container in their hands to the right. Keep doing this until everyone's water returns to them.
8. Take that water home, leave it at room temperature in a quiet place. Use it to drink, cook with or wash and see if you notice anything that arises in your relationship with that water.

I myself have stories about how Moon Water has helped my children and me. Not "scientific" evidence, of course, but it works for us. Such stories are common in the communities with whom I interact.

If water is impacted by intention, what might symmetrical crystallization signify or correlate with? How exactly has the water changed and how does it affect those who drink, cook or wash with it? Since our human bodies are 70-90% water (depending on age and other factors) and water comprises a huge percentage of the weight and mass of most life forms on the planet, how do we affect them or they us with "intention"? What do we do to others when we project hate and anger; love and compassion? What do we do to the planet we all depend on for survival?

How does the jargon we use in activist culture impact us? Since I was a child people around me have debated the use of violence-laden words to describe good works. "The *war* on poverty." "*Armed* with this information we can ..." "The *struggle* continues." These words have both an emotional and physical impact on us. Indeed, they may have several impacts on us. If "the struggle continues" evokes memories of momentary victories by the world's revolutionaries and recollections of celebration, honour and empowerment maybe that's not so bad. However, if we're in a room full of people who have differing reactions to, experiences with or understandings of the words, what is happening to their biology with their use? Do activists have a different relationship with some words or some jargon than other folks?

I'm not alone in feeling uncomfortable with the uses of words like *anti*-racism, *anti*-colonialism and *anti*-imperialism in our movements. I certainly appreciate the sentiments but a term like *anti-colonial* not only centralizes colonization in our work and identities, it also doesn't speak to what we aspire to achieve. I prefer terms like *indigenization* or *indigenizing the commons* because they speak, in part, to the vision. Anishinaabeg scholar and activist Leanne Simpson uses words like *cultural renewal* and *revival* to describe what First Nations activists advocate and work toward. In light of Emoto's and Radin's work, we might wonder what impact the words we use in activist settings have on our physiology and mindset.

Teachings I have received in the Yoruba traditions also hold that our thoughts, feelings and words play a role shaping our physical reality. We are warned to be careful of the words we speak, particularly aloud, as they have conjuring power. When I was singing with groups in the community and even whenever I recorded music I was very careful with both my lyrics and the intent behind them. I wanted my music to lift spirits and bring joy, not make people sick or angry. Similarly, with my stories, my intent is to generate more compassion, hope and gratitude in the world. In responding to a 2010 interview for Black Coffee Poet's blog, I wrote:

> ... everything I write tends to have positive, happy or uplifting endings (even non-fic) because I care about leaving people hopeful. Words, whether spoken or written, have conjuring power. Why conjure up more negativity? What purpose does that serve?
>
> At the same time I don't believe that being in denial about some scary stuff going on in the world is useful. I think our hope and positivity actually have greater impact when we hold on to them in the context of some tough realizations and difficult history. If life was la-di-da easy and happy all the time what would our hope and positivity count for? It's in coming out of challenge, trauma and tragedy that we truly appreciate love, peace and laughter.

Later in the interview I was asked, "What role do you see poetry having in activism? How can poetry get more than a quarter of a page in a magazine (if at all) and be used as more than an opener at events?" This is an excerpt from my answer:

> I think that what can make poetry and other artistic disciplines powerful in terms of articulating visions, encouraging actions, educating, etc. is that they can inspire us to allow love to motivate what we think, say and do. I've heard activists say they do what they do because they hate and are angry about something. My response to them is that there's enough of that in the world and look where it's gotten us. It doesn't take a particularly creative or talented person to spread more hatred, anger and fear. I ask what's behind those feelings. Fear is the source emotion for hatred and anger. Fear is based in a realistic concern that our basic needs aren't going to be met. And love is a basic human need, as essential as food and water to our survival. Offer love as a motivation for forming community or

123

challenging injustice or writing and see what happens. Act like you care for life – all life – and see how many people start to listen to the message. I think the activists and academics that role model caring concern have the most sustainable successes AND derive the most joy from their work.

So, poetry and other forms of artistic expression can be very helpful in terms of movement building and inspiring social change.

Even if you find the arguments for "energetic-based" connections less than convincing, there are other reasons for basing our activism, in fact all of our behaviours, on love.

CHAPTER EIGHT: SHAPE-SHIFTING TRICKSTERS

This chapter will out the shape-shifters and tricksters lurking within the research and its interpretations so we can better apply the knowledge to our social justice work. To some extent we've discussed cautions, critiques and limitations already and they will be expanded upon here. I recognize that some activists can be quite hostile to spirituality but I have attempted to tease out where gems of wisdom or practices from Indigenous and other cultures might be useful in terms of contextualizing the information. At the same time, I have refrained from exploring deeply spiritual principles because 1) you don't have to be spiritual to benefit from this information, 2) that is not the purpose of this book, 3) I'm not wise enough to provide spiritual teachings and 4) I trust that people can and will follow up on whatever spiritual knowledge they feel they need from various other sources that exist in the world. I've discussed Indigenous and other knowledges in limited ways in an attempt to illustrate the wisdom, rationality and logic of these lifeways. I feel this is necessary because such knowledge and practices have been denigrated over the centuries and that has caused much pain and suffering for too long. As stated previously, it is not my intent to convert anyone to any particular spiritual tradition.

Although I've shared a lot of this hard science information in workshops, speaking gigs and other writings, no one has yet asked me some major questions I have asked myself. This might be because it takes time to process all this information but I'm sure sooner or later such questions will be asked, so I'll address them here. The questions are: Why trust new and emerging science that comes out of the dominant, colonial paradigm? Why accept the findings of a knowledge tradition that has, for at least 500 years, rationalized hetero-patriarchy, racism and colonialism? Why accept the conclusions of a field of knowledge that has produced weapons of war without apology, justifies environmental destruction and benefits from the genocide of Indigenous peoples around the world?

As I mentioned in the Introduction, both left and right brain thinking have the capacity to lead us to the same place. Similarly, there are philosophical frameworks that have already arrived at the location where the new science is taking us. The science has helped me understand ancient teachings in a new way and sometimes affirmed what has been known by wise people for centuries. These facts, along with my personal experiences of applying this knowledge in my life have led me to "believe" in it, so to speak. None of this means, however, that we can throw caution to the wind when we interpret or act on the hard science knowledge. What we do with this new knowledge has a lot to do with our system of values. The framework in which we seek, interpret and utilize knowledge has significant implications. For example, we can use fire to burn or to cook, depending on what we value and the outcomes we desire.

Recent hard science discoveries can be used in ways that can either take us farther from the socially just world we want to co-create or it can take us closer. There are hard science discoveries and new technologies that emerge every day that I have not dealt with in this book. That's partly because of my limited understanding of some of the science but mostly it's because many of these technologies and discoveries conflict with what I hold to be the values of a socially just world. I find the ways we can genetically alter our food, create new pharmaceuticals and make more effective weapons, to be counterproductive to the work we do as activists. Clearly, the values engraved into my worldview have enabled me to choose the science that I explore. It also impacts my interpretation of the findings and their uses.

In sum, we don't need to fear knowledge itself; we need to reframe the paradigm that births it so it becomes useful to our social justice aspirations. The new science discussed here confirms that our vision of a socially just world is not only desirable and achievable but also intrinsic to individual and social wellbeing. We are wired for social justice. Further, I would argue strongly that contextualizing new knowledge in relational frameworks is 1) inherent to the science itself and 2) conducive to using it in ways that support social justice and sustainable community building.

We can and must (if we are to survive as a human species) re-contextualize this emerging knowledge into a paradigm that is consistent and compatible with the knowledge itself. As mentioned previously, emerging discoveries become random facts unless they are contextualized within a worldview. Once contextualized within a paradigm (along with its system of values), information is used in a way that is consistent with and serves the perpetuation of the ultimate values system. So, we must ask ourselves, which worldview do we want to perpetuate? Of all the philosophical frameworks available to human societies, of all the wisdom teachings throughout all time, which allow us to make the best uses of this new information?

If your worldview or your core beliefs don't allow you to imagine cooperative, compassionate communities because you believe that humans are inherently competitive and selfish, would you apply scientific knowledge towards building a world that is different from what we now live in? Of course not. If your activist worldview holds that your rage at the system doesn't impact your children, your neighbours or the plants and animals; if you believe your anger is righteous and necessary to motivate you to work toward revolutionary change, why would you strive to manage and minimize your anger? If you believe that anger is what galvanizes you and others to take action to transform society, why would you cultivate compassion and encourage others to do the same? If you don't believe that activism can be grounded in peace, calm and gratitude why would you cultivate those feelings in yourself and others, now or ever?

There are many wisdom traditions that have developed rituals, ceremonies and practices that have enabled practitioners to conclude that we are all related; that we impact and are impacted by all, that everything in the world is in constant transition and movement and that individualism is a fiction. They may not have framed or explained this knowledge within the language of materialist, reductionist science but the information was known.

If you must discard spirituality from the discussion, ask this: from a social justice perspective, which paradigm makes more sense in terms of the world you want to create? Materialism or relationality? Right or left brain? Do we need to choose only one among two? Can't we draw on both knowledge ways (and possibly others) to help us understand, utilize and grow new knowledge for the purposes of creating a better world? Can these knowledge traditions be "in relationship"?

To my mind, left brained, materialist thinking has discovered or compiled many wonderful truths about the world. It has served some useful purposes such as adding to our collection of healing modalities and technologies, even though it has denied, devalued and ignored, as well as stolen from other knowledge systems. There are scholars who have demonstrated that much of what today passes as Eurocentric knowledge is based on knowledges originally developed in Asia, Africa and the Middle East. Europeans learned algebra and geometry from Arab and Middle Eastern peoples. Many modern architectural technologies are rooted in Arab, Middle Eastern and African traditions. Gunpowder and printing originated in Asia. The healing properties of Willow Bark that gave birth to aspirin was discovered by Indigenous peoples of the Americas. So, in fact, much of the knowledge we consider Eurocentric is not purely so anyway.

The fact that White supremacists have created and institutionalized the mythology that the vast majority of useful knowledge came from the European-descended scientists and innovators does not make it fact. Much of what we consider mainstream science has been de-cultured, decontextualized and re-storied.

Personally, my health has been restored at various points during my lifetime due to surgery, antibiotics and other materialist interventions –

what most would consider to be part of that Eurocentric system. Sure, other treatments had a significant role to play. In fact, it's entirely possible that other healing approaches, if I'd been immersed in another culture, would have allowed me to avoid my health problems altogether. It's also probable that the lifestyle I've been living in a world dominated by materialist, colonial ways of thinking made me sick to begin with. Nevertheless, materialistic knowledge can be re-contextualized to better serve our collective needs. The crucial questions for me are: 1) Is the context in which this knowledge is developed and used the best possible one available to us? 2) Are there other knowledge ways that are equally or more useful to us in terms of maintaining wellness? 3) Are there other frameworks of accumulating and applying knowledge that promote wellbeing? Clearly, this book, among other resources, demonstrates the answer is *yes*.

To my mind there is nothing wrong with taking the materialistic knowledge that we have and putting it to good use. From what I understand of integrative medicine approaches to healthcare I'm not alone in advocating this. In theory, integrative medicine suggests that drawing on any and all healing traditions is desirable in the quest to restore someone to wellness. (Note that wellness is not the absence of illness.) That is why health care professionals increasingly see acupuncture, herbal medicines and meditation as "complementary" to other more conventional treatments for many forms of illness.

Of course, many might point out that the ways in which medicine is "integrated" in practice prioritizes and centralizes Eurocentric, materialist approaches over others. Not to mention that energetic forms of healing are not always covered by health insurance in Canada or the U.S, thus making them inaccessible to many. These are issues that certainly need to be addressed. Regardless, the theory (if not the current practice) of integrative medicine might serve as a model for a kind of "integrated" approach to social activism.

If we are not living in a material world but are living in a world where energy determines the behavior of matter or a world that is completely energetic and particles don't exist, what are the implications for our activism, relationships, and how we establish sustainable communities? If we can make changes in our world and to each other through our thoughts and feelings as well as actions, what are the implications?

Careful about New Ageism

As someone of Cherokee and African American ancestry, it has long been a source of annoyance to me when New Age gurus declare that any individual's or community's problems and difficulties are the result of flawed mindsets. This implies that it is our flawed and erroneous ways of

128

thinking that are solely responsible for creating and inviting problems -- even disasters.

I once attended a talk given by a married (White) couple that offers couples' counseling to others. Their approach shocked and angered me. The male half of the duo shared that his background had been in counseling survivors of domestic violence in South Africa. He said his approach to this work was to help the women understand that they had made decisions to attract and enable their abusive partners. Consequently, in making different decisions these women could attract healthy relationships. This, he believed, was key to helping the women heal. The duo took the same general approach to couples counseling, asking their clients to acknowledge and take responsibility as individuals for whatever showed up in their relationship and in their lives generally. This, they believed, was key to resolving all the world's problems.

While this all sounded good in terms of encouraging people to take responsibility for their situations and their personal decisions it seemed like a blame-the-victim approach to me. It also seemed a rather individualistic response to problems that have, in large part, been collectively created. I questioned the duo.

"So if I'm a black woman walking in a park and some racist white guy decides to attack me does that mean I'm responsible?"

In the conversation that followed, this couple maintained that in this hypothetical situation I was very much responsible. Ultimately, they claimed, I had conspired with the spirit of my attacker at a "soul level" to arrange for that assault because we both needed that incident in our lives in order to help us grow to the next level. The implication of this type of thinking is that children born with disabilities, victims of natural disasters and people who become ill are singularly responsible for their plight. There are some in my networks who believe this is an inaccurate and twisted interpretation of the concept of karma, designed to alleviate White Guilt and protect the current social order. In any case, this is where social justice advocates, some of whom may be very spiritual people, must part ways with some New Age philosophies.

Billions of people have taken centuries to create paradigms, practices and institutions that rationalize and reproduce inequality, be it racism, colonialism, classism, ablism, ageism, heterosexism, patriarchy, etc. These inequalities and systems of oppression were collectively produced over centuries. Why is it those who now bear the brunt of these ways of thinking and doing, those who are directly harmed by it, suddenly become solely responsible for its appearance in their lives? How can it be that collectively created and maintained problems are solved at an individual level through simply changing our personal mindset?

If we look again at the Kewaywin First Nation example, how is it those children, who have been poisoned by radioactive uranium, become responsible for their plight? How is it that the rest of us are absolved of responsibility for them? Even if we didn't play a direct role in creating the problem, can we not take some responsibility (response ability) for making choices that contribute to creating a society where such atrocities don't happen? Are we in any way directly or indirectly benefiting from a system that created this atrocity? Is our personal healing journey intertwined with that of others? Assuming that we didn't know about Keewaywin before, what are our responsibilities now that we do know? Can helping others be separated from our personal spiritual or moral development? Isn't helping others crucial to our own wellness?

Many wisdom teachers like to tell us that world peace is achieved one person at a time; that until each and every one of us can achieve some form of inner peace we will not enjoy a peaceful world. This is, of course, important for social justice advocates to understand and live. The question for me is, how do we achieve that sense of inner peace? Can we achieve it for and by ourselves, in isolation, meditating on mountaintops or only among the like-minded? Or does our self-development inherently, intrinsically involve Our Relations? How do we separate ourselves from other living beings in this world? Can it be that allowing our relationships to help us be and do better is what furthers our development as individuals and a species? How would you be able to practice the generosity, kindness and gratitude that contribute to your wellbeing and spiritual development if you didn't have others to relate to?

My teachings, life experience and spiritual guidance, for whatever they are worth, have suggested that focusing on your own personal development cannot be a solitary process because you need others to support your spiritual evolution. You can't evolve in isolation. While I believe engaging in practices that look inward and attempt to fortify your connection to Spirit are essential to spiritual development and I recognize that, at some level, your spiritual development is inherently and intrinsically helpful to others, intended or not, I don't believe that collectively-created social problems can be overcome by an individual on a personal quest. At some level our survival and spiritual growth is interconnected and inter-dependent. As we have seen, our capacity to make decisions that enhance our spiritual growth as individuals is connected to our relationships as well as our physical, mental and emotional states. It's also connected to a host of other influences over space and time.

My spiritual development is not disconnected from yours. It's not disconnected from the ancestors. It's not disconnected from the Earth's wellbeing. It's not disconnected from the Sun or the centre of the galaxy, for that matter. Solutions that focus on individual self-development, whether through meditation or prayer or shifting mindset, are incomplete.

This is easy for the activist to understand but difficult for some New Agers. At the same time, what is referred to as "healing" in Indigenous cultures is not always well accepted by social justice advocates, who believe that solutions to the world's ills must be collectively driven and that once society changes we individuals who comprise it will automatically become well. Sorry, but we still have to take responsibilities as individuals for how we interact with the world. There needs to be a balance of individual and collective responsibility.

None of information in this book advocates for forms of activism that are self-involved. Nor does it advocate an exclusive focus on social transformation. Your relationships impact you and you impact your relationships. Social and personal transformation is inter-connected, interdependent and related. In this framework making changes that reflect and make use of relationality are not easy. Why? Because we don't have unilinear control over … well, anything.

First of all, as we have clearly seen, we're impacted by both our internal and external environments, which interact. I won't belabor this point here because I've been making it throughout the book. Diet, air quality and the toxicity of people around you all impact your capacity to transform either yourself or society. Your thoughts and feelings are only responsible for 30% of your wellbeing says biologist Dr. Bruce Lipton. I have no idea how such statistics are determined but they do remind us that we are impacted by both our physical and social environments; environments that are co-created not just by us but by many billions of people – sometimes over several generations. Environments also result from processes and happenings are derived from both human and non-human intervention. Non-human influences on our environment include the changes of season, the day/night rhythms or cosmic impacts on the Earth's magnetic field.

We also have to understand that the external environment includes the past as well. As someone whose ancestors were enslaved I've come to understand how their physical, mental and emotional stresses were passed on in our family history. The experience of enslavement and racism shaped my family dynamics and my individual sense of self. Like many others, my family has struggled with domestic violence, sexual abuse and other issues no one likes to talk about, much less experience. It is obvious to me that the history of being enslaved had a role to play in fostering these unhealthy behaviours.

I have no doubt that my ancestors' enslavement has impacted me at every level of my being. I have childhood memories of emotions I felt while reading the stories of enslaved people; listening to beloved family members speak about their experiences in the Jim Crow state of Virginia and; being taunted and beaten up as a child when sent to integrate a formerly all-white school outside of Philadelphia. I felt the fear, anger and stress of knowing not only that these terrible things had happened to me and my loved ones but that they could still happen to my children and others I cared about because the racism that justified genocide and slavery are still embedded in the dominant culture's worldview and institutions.

That fear, anger and stress were among many feelings that elicited biochemical reactions in my body and shaped my physical, mental and emotional self. This in turn has shaped my perception of the world; my roles, responsibilities and understanding of limitations within it. And these perceptions are among many that are rooted in my ancestors' lives.

Luckily no one in my family had to go to residential school but it is quite clear in literature and oral accounts that the legacy of that experience also impacts many generations of Indigenous families on Turtle Island.

Even someone who doesn't consider her/himself to be a spiritual person can acknowledge how relationships with parents have impacted her/his perceptions, values and behaviours. If they are wise enough they will understand that their parents were similarly impacted by grandparents, who were in turn impacted by great grandparents and so on, back multiple generations. We may be unaware of role modeling or rejecting perceptions, emotions and thinking that originated centuries ago. We may have internalized messages that come from ancestors we may never have heard of.

Science is increasingly demonstrating that ancestral perceptions, values and memory are passed on not only through socialization but also biologically. Our genetics and other biological functions are shaped at a very early age by our social and family environments *and* before birth by ancestral experiences. We internalize messages about who we are, who we are not, why we are (or are not) loved unconditionally as well as which expressed feelings, thoughts and behaviours will keep us alive and thriving. Certainly, how we are nurtured (or not) will impact our physical, mental and emotional development. Molecules of thought and emotion impact our body chemistry, which in turn impacts our physical development down to our very genes and then gets passed to the next generation. The process moves in reverse as well; our body chemistry impacts our thoughts and feelings in a continuous cycle. Add to this the external environmental influences outside of our body (physical and social), which further influence our perceptions, feelings and biology, and we get a better idea of the complex web of relationships affecting every aspect of our being.

As previously noted, the nature versus nurture argument is over and has been for some decades, despite the denial of many sectors of society. We now realize what Indigenous peoples have known for centuries: that we cannot be separated from either our physical or *social* environments; they *both* shape our perceptions, biology and consequently behaviours. Of course, the reverse is also true, our perceptions, physicality and behaviours shape the environment and society. Hence, we have another compelling reason to heal ancestral relationships in our quest to heal the planet and society.

Another reason for the complexity of changing your mindset and emotional set points is the fact that much of what you think and feel is subconscious, which means you're not aware of it at the moment you think and feel it. Lipton says that 95% of what we think and feel every day is subconscious. As we discussed earlier, a large part of your subconscious is programmed before birth. The bio-chemicals running through your mother's bloodstream when you were in the uterus influenced the structures and processes of your body. After birth, for the first six to seven years of life, your brain pretty much did nothing more than download information from the environment you lived and (hopefully) played in. The predominant brain state of small children is Theta. This is the brain state of people who are hypnotized. It's a passive state where you are very open to suggestion, where you are learning and internalizing information. There is no judgment or critical thinking going on when you are in a Theta state.

So, for example, if you were programmed early in life to experience the world as a dangerous, unloving and lonely place that programming basically runs your life 95% of the time until you do something about it. If you were programmed to believe you are in any way inferior to others, that is the script running in the background of your mind. If you were taught through your experiences that you are unlovable or undeserving, every moment that you are not consciously telling yourself something else, your thinking will revert to that default setting.

It is not our conscious thinking that needs to shift in order to initiate an inner and outer transformation but our *unconscious* thoughts. More than that, the subconscious mind doesn't learn in the same way our conscious mind does. The subconscious learns mostly while in the Theta state. This is a state that people achieve in meditation, under hypnosis or going into and out of sleep. As discussed earlier, you also go into a receptive Theta state when you are sitting in front of the TV, a horrifying revelation when you realize how much junk your unconscious mind can absorb, particularly children who don't have the capacity to think critically. There are other times when we can deliberately achieve a Theta state, such as in many First Nations and other Indigenous ceremonies. The challenge is to aware of and prepared for when we're in that state and do something while in it to shift our subconscious thinking.

So, the good news is that we don't have to wait for positive emotional states to suddenly impact us. We can cultivate these emotions and the healthful benefits they generate for us and Our Relations through fantasy and imagination, or by simply focusing our thoughts, calling up specific memories or other activities. The more this can be done while in a Theta frame of mind, the more effective it will be.

It's important, however, to understand that, just as people don't all react uniformly to the same drug, therapies or treatments, not everyone will respond the same way at the same pace to methods of changing unhelpful core beliefs. Consequently, I believe that it's important to experiment and see what you are most comfortable with; what works satisfactorily. I recommend starting with seeing what you can do for yourself without spending money. There are so many hucksters out there practicing techniques they don't fully understand and sometimes it can be very risky. Or you may spend a pile of money on a technique that doesn't work as well as something you can do for free in the comfort of your own home. There are methods like Emotional Freedom Techniques, self-hypnosis and meditation practices that you can learn to practice for yourself using resources found online or in public libraries.

I also wonder about collectively changing core beliefs. If core beliefs initially are established through socialization, can a group of people work together to "reprogram" each other? My experience with ceremony suggests the answer is yes, provided folks are clear and intentional about what they're doing. I also feel that systematizing practices in community and creating social circles dedicated to supporting individual transitions is crucial to social transformations.

Its further important to understand that changing core beliefs takes time. How much time involves so many internal and external factors related to you and your specific context that it's impossible to put a timeline on such a transformation just as it is for someone to tell you when you should be over your grief at the death of a loved one. But for biological reasons alone, shifting subconscious beliefs is difficult because, as you recall, our cells and organs become physically structured to accommodate our ways of thinking and feeling. Nevertheless, it can be done.

If you do decide to embark on such a transformation, it's healthy to remember that you're a human being having a human experience in a "material" world – or at least a world that simulates materiality. Whether you believe your spirit chose to come here or you were created by a Deity or are an accident of random evolutionary forces, you won't transcend the human experience. Challenges of your own making, and otherwise, will continue to come and go in your life. The question is how do you responsibly respond to them? How do you respond in a way that allows you to extract the maximum meaning and joy from your life experiences? How do *we* respond to them collectively?

Dealing with "Negative" Emotions

As we've noted, emotions related to death, illness, injury and danger are a necessary part of our lives. We need to feel afraid when threatened with danger so we can take appropriate steps to stay safe. Yet there are negative emotions that we need to minimize in our lives for the sake of our personal and collective wellbeing.

The Dalai Lama, among other spiritual teachers, has spoken and written about the different types of negative emotions that we can experience. Sadness, depression and grief can often diminish when we talk about our feelings with sympathetic listeners or take actions that allow us to experience these feelings until they dissipate. But there is another category of emotions termed "afflictive" that are not diminished simply because we talk about them, and especially not if we act upon them. In fact, allowing emotions like anger, jealousy or hatred to direct our thoughts, words, and deeds can wreak havoc for us. We've already examined the science behind this. Anger, which is particularly relevant to activists, impacts our wellbeing and enjoyment of life. It impacts the taste of our food, the quality of our sleep and our relationships to loved ones.

It is absolutely impossible to achieve social justice through actions based in anger. It's impossible, as we've seen, to make wise decisions when stuck in anger. It's impossible to feel compassion and anger at the same time, the science says. It's impossible to create a climate of trust and collegiality when in the throes of anger. Managing anger and diminishing its impact in our lives is crucial to the struggle for social justice. Period. It is no longer an acceptable excuse for activists to righteously claim anger as their motivator.

Yes, injustice requires a serious, firm and consistent response but you don't have to be angry to respond to injustice. In fact, considering the science we've reviewed on what anger does to your mind and body, your response to injustice is clearly more effective when not fueled by anger.

By definition, being an activist for social justice requires the kind of emotional maturity that manages anger, hatred and fear. This is a responsibility. Furthermore, it is only through intentional, consistent management that we can diminish our anger. No, you won't ever find yourself immune to anger. You will not escape that human condition. But you can strive to minimize how often, how long and how quickly you experience anger. You can certainly control how you act when feeling angry.

I like to use the visual of the sine wave to talk about how to deal with negative emotions. A sine wave is the oscillation of energy. The illustration in the "Depression" graphic represents a vibration, back and forth. Energy must vibrate, must move. It's frequency, length and other characteristics change as it changes states.

We've established that our thoughts and emotions are forms of energy. If you can imagine that the peaks above the line in the represent your positive emotions and those below, your negative emotions, you can see that a healthy emotional life requires an ongoing crisscrossing of that line, moving above and below at differing rates depending on what life brings you in the moment. You won't avoid ever falling below the line because – well, that's life. What you don't want to do is get stuck below the line, as in because that's very unpleasant and impacts you in various negative ways. What folks normally strive to do in life is to remain above the line because it feels better. But that isn't possible or ultimately, as we've discussed, desirable because it robs us of opportunities to grow.

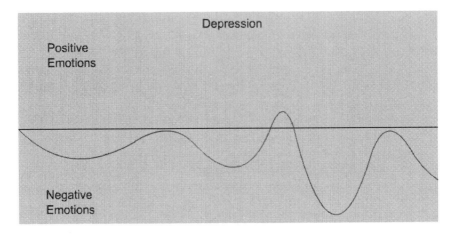

A participant in one of my workshops was a practitioner of Chinese forms of medicine and she noted that in her tradition they have a diagnosis of "too much happiness." I'm not sure what this refers to specifically. It might be about repressing and avoiding negativity or about constantly chasing bright lights and positive experiences in a constant (and I would assume frustrating) attempt to remain in an ongoing state of emotional bliss. In any case, most people think the challenge of transforming themselves into optimists and positivists might be to spend more time above the line than below it. For those of us stuck in depression, anger or other forms of negativity that's certainly true. However, I like to think that the challenge is actually about raising the line, as you'll see in the "Raise Your Game" illustration on the next page

If you think of the difference between an amateur soccer player and a professional one, you'll note that both experiences involve winning games and losing them; playing well and not playing well. So what separates the amateur from the professional? The quality of play. Before my youngest son could enter the ranks of professional soccer he had to "up his game." It didn't mean he would never lose a game or never play badly again. Turning professional was about experiencing a higher level of excellence and a deeper sense of joy and accomplishment in playing his favorite sport.

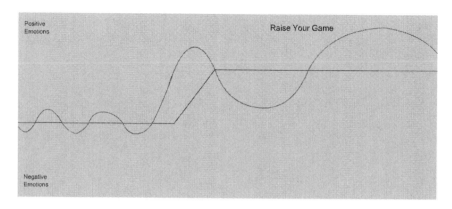

(I'm sure he appreciated the extra money too.) My point is that attempting to avoid negativity is a futile exercise. Attempting to raise your overall game where you can manage difficulty, learn from it and bounce back is probably much more doable.

In the grip of fear, anger and negativity you lose your grounding and capacity to think clearly. You radiate negativity. The physical structure of your body is altered to produce more negativity. When in this state what do you have to contribute to the vision of a society grounded in compassion, cooperation and optimism? Yes, you have a right to be angry. So what? How does acknowledging that get us anywhere? How does justifying our anger as a rational and human response to injustice advance our cause? As mentioned, there's a difference between *feeling* and *being* angry.

Unfortunately, this book cannot go into the many ways that you can change your relationship to anger and other negative emotions. What it offers for those who believe that anger is an appropriate motivator for social action are questions to begin that process. Exploring your anger brings greater self-awareness and from there you can shift unhelpful core beliefs and the behaviours they motivate. Hopefully, if you have an issue with anger you will find a way to manage it in helpful ways and there are many resources out there to draw upon. So, as a start ask yourself: what is the value of anger, especially when contrasted with compassion, patience and tolerance? What purpose does it serve? Who does it harm? How does it harm? Does it ever help? Are there other emotional states that better help you achieve the long-term outcomes you are looking for?

When it's not possible to single-handedly change your environment to alleviate the negative emotions you experience, my advice, trite though it may sound, would be to change your relationship to your feelings. Feel the pain, anger and fear. Maintain an awareness of your feelings but don't identify with them. In other words don't *be* an angry, fearful or hateful person. Be a person who is feeling these things in the moment. Trust that every situation, like it or not, shifts. What you're experiencing is temporary.

Don't confuse your situation with your identity. If you want to be useful to others who need your help and support, find a way go grow spiritually from your challenges.

Dr. Izzeldin Abulaish lost two daughters and a niece when an Israeli bomb hit his Gaza home within a year of losing his wife to cancer. Yet he was able to write a book called *I Shall Not Hate* for the purpose of helping others. I believe that each of us, as activists, can likewise find a way to turn our recovery from trauma and adversity into a way of uplifting the collective spirit. That is the subject of our next chapter.

CHAPTER NINE: ACTIVIST FORCES

Now that we have ingested these hard science facts, what do we, as activists, do with them? How does this knowledge shift or change our lives? our activist practice? our relationships? our work in communities? our visions? our paradigms?

Surely a collective process would come up with many more creative responses to these questions than I can muster here and I'm anxious to see that happen. Certainly one's individual and collective context will influence responses. The most important question I feel this information raises is: how might our work be impacted by a paradigm shift that involves a change of focus from materialism to relationality?

This has been a difficult question to answer for artists, activists and community workers who have come to my workshops. It's very common for people exposed for the first time to the information in this book to consider it relevant to "self-care," and it is, but it's also much more. One activist in a workshop believed this information provides no valid reason for questioning left-wing political paradigms and instead suggested such frameworks only needed a bit of "tweaking." I didn't have time to question her as to why she suggested this but I disagree.

For about a year and a half I worked on an anti-colonial film series project conceptualized by a group of academic activists in partnership with community artists. The idea was to produce a film series exploring how colonization had been and still was impacting a variety of racialized communities as well as looking at decolonizing efforts within those communities. Our group was representative of various racialized groups, including First Nations. I had initially been invited to perform opening ceremonies for the group's meetings, which took place every few months. I was asked *not* to do a traditional ceremony from a specific nation but to perform an opening that might speak to the multiplicity of cultures, backgrounds, belief systems, life choices, experiences and so on in the room. I accepted the challenge.

My openings provided opportunities for me to share information I was learning as I researched this book. Examples of exercises I offered people were to list five things for which they were grateful or take a moment to envision the best-case outcome of their work. I might have had them do some breathing while I sang. I explained the science behind what I was doing. I took care not to alienate people who did not share a spiritual worldview. "You don't have to believe in the Great Spirit or God or whatever to get the benefits of this exercise," I remember saying once. "Even science proves that five hours of being intentionally grateful can boost your immune system, enhance your creativity and sharpen your intellect." People who wanted to use the opportunity in a spiritual way had that opportunity but I believe I also showed respect for atheists and agnostics, whether they outed themselves or not, because I genuinely honour them and value their contributions to our movements.

The Indigenous participants in the group, judging from their comments, found the openings perfectly compatible and consistent with their cultural beliefs and practices. The point for the Indigenous participants, as I understand it, is that they wanted, first of all, a group process that enabled them to feel grounded and connected to each other so as to enhance their work together. Secondly, they saw in the opening an opportunity to connect to the Great Spirit. (These reasons are not ranked in order of importance but are, of course, infused into each other.)

Unfortunately, not all of the project participants appreciated the idea of an opening ceremony and many did not attend. After a year and a half I was told by the group's lead that my services were no longer required. The Coordinating Committee (CC) had had a discussion and decided the openings were either unnecessary or detrimental to the working process. Some of the people participating in that discussion had never even attended an opening and maintained "ceremonial processes" were experienced by them as a form of colonization. The two First Nations members of the CC were not present at the meeting where this decision was made.

When an email announcement informed the larger group that the opening ceremony had been discontinued, the First Nations members were very upset. They invited me to a phone conference where they expressed their hurt and shock that in a project ultimately aiming to facilitate decolonization, one of their strategies for doing this had been nixed. They made a plan to address the issue, sensitive to the fact that everyone involved in the project had been harmed by colonization, though not all in the same way. We wanted to explore how our differing experiences with colonization and White supremacy had not only impacted our varied decolonization strategies but our relationships across communities.

The discussion within the group continues and I'm no longer part of the project so I don't know how the issues are being managed or if a resolution is at hand. I recognize that this conflict can provide an opportunity to learn and grow our relationships. Or, maybe, and sadly, it won't turn out that way. But I have hope.

In any case, my point here is to illustrate how our paradigms impact our visions, goals, strategies and processes. If your paradigm does not value collective processes that recognize and cultivate spiritual/energetic connection; if you feel threatened by hearing that for many communities ceremony is a crucial part of their decolonizing process, then what hope do we have of working as allies or in solidarity with each other? Our paradigms impact how we work together to make the world better, even assuming we share a general vision of the world we aspire to create.

Everything flows from worldview. We don't necessarily all need to share the same worldview in order to work together. In fact, one could argue that such a requirement defeats the purpose of collective organizing, where you actually value differentness for its capacity to enhance the quality and effectiveness of your work. However, we know that there is a level at which differing worldviews are fundamentally incompatible. There are worldviews that don't serve the survival of the human species, or other life forms for that matter. I think that social justice movements have come to a place where we need to recognize that the "religion" of materiality is not going to take us to the next level of struggle.

This absolutely does not mean that we all have to share a *spiritual* worldview. Left-brained science seems to be taking us all to the same relational place. If we all end up in useful places why does it matter whether we follow the path of science or the path of a wisdom tradition? Is it possible to separate them anyway, as many nation-states claim to have done in recent history? (I think that Christian and Jewish values informing the dominant culture's worldview, institutions and practices are not apparent and/or denied by many who are invested in the status quo.) Aren't we always constantly building on each other's knowledges, as well as the wisdom of the land and Our Relations?

This is not an argument for cultural appropriation. Nor is it one for the amalgamation of church and state. It is an argument for reclaiming, reviving and reinvigorating culturally and historically appropriate paradigms that better serve humanity.

Compassion, generosity and gratitude are necessary to the flourishing of life. Interacting with and respecting the integrity of other species on the planet, as well as the planet Herself, is crucial to our collective wellbeing. In fact, these are all crucial to our very survival as a human species. The new paradigm recognizes that our social progress impacts and is impacted by our physical evolution. In fact, our physical evolution as a species is influenced by our collective intent and how we act on it. This is profound. Of course, the same is true of our social evolution and both our physical and social evolution are *in relationship*.

Regardless of which hemisphere of the brain dominates within any given individual, regardless of the language of expression, isn't it possible that our various visions of a socially just world can be completely compatible?

For a skeletal outline of a vision of a socially just world, I refer you to an article published on Rabble: "Community, Relationship Framework and Implications for Activism".[84] In sum, this vision is one where healthy sustainable communities recognize our inter-connectedness with and inter-dependence on each other as well as the other species of the planet; where individual wellbeing is understood to be crucial to that of the community and community wellbeing is crucial to that of the individual; and where relationships among communities contribute to globalized wellbeing. I don't own the vision outlined in that article. It comes out of ancient teachings as well as out of interacting with colleagues, friends and ancestors. Nevertheless, if we can agree that a relationship framework is intrinsic to our vision, then there are crucial implications for our strategies and tactics.

As someone who grew up in the midst of the Civil Rights, American Indian and Brown Power Movements, I recall what made organizations like the Black Panthers (for whom I sold newspapers in my childhood) powerful and dangerous in the eyes of authorities, and admirable to me. It was the way in which they won over the hearts and minds of their communities by enacting self-empowerment with child breakfast programs, senior escort services and free health care – all implemented without a penny of government funding.

We can discuss how effective or not these movements were at achieving their goals but regardless of which side we come down on in the debate, I think most of us recognize that protest isn't sufficient to usher in the kind of changes we seek. Besides, who has the time to participate in ten demonstrations a week? Who has the energy to negotiate ongoing coalition-building with the myriad of social change groups out there? What are the implications of our dependence on protest tactics for differently-abled people? For women with children? For people living outside of urban centres who can't afford regular travel? Who ends up playing leadership roles in our movements when it centralizes protest and mass action as the focal point of social change? Why do we count attendance at our activities as a measure of success but fail to make significant efforts to measure shifts in thinking of those both present and not?

Don't get me wrong. I believe that many protests and actions are useful, helpful, and downright necessary. There are moments when you just have to protect land from development; defend Our Relations (and the

---

[84] " http://rabble.ca/news/2010/07/community-%E2%80%98relationship-framework%E2%80%99-and-implications-activism

food chain) from industrial pollutants; protect lives from state and corporate violence; advocate for consumer boycotts, divestment and sanctions that weaken genocidal corporations, and take advantage of international scrutiny to make a point (or several points) at key historical junctures.

I'm also well aware that many activists are involved in community building activities such as providing services, advocating for individuals in crisis, training, awareness-raising and so on. While we acknowledge that crisis services (especially government funded ones) don't fix the fundamental problems that arise our of our colonized/capitalist political economy (and it can be argued, these services may actually exacerbate dependency and disempowerment) we still understand that in building relationships with people we are able to engage their hearts and minds and cultivate growing support for our varied goals and ultimate vision. Not to mention that we, ourselves, are transformed in the act of working together for change.

Sometimes, though, I wonder whether there is an imbalance between protesting, with all that entails, and facilitating community empowerment, in which protesting gets more time and attention. As a form of resistance, is protest the highest aspiration of community empowerment? I further wonder, what is the most effective balance of resources allocated to, for example, organizing protests versus nurturing a shift in thinking and preparing for the inevitable demise of capitalism? Are there some alternatives to protest that might more effectively support the person-by-person transformations that need to happen to accomplish our goals and establish the vision we share?

I have some suggestions in this regard. As activists we excel at harnessing resources for actions, education and legal defense funds. How about allocating some of those resources to community empowerment? For example, how about supporting community gardening? Or enabling groups to purchase eco-friendly vehicles to be used for community purposes? Investing in our own renewable energy sources to power our activities and community spaces? How about supporting collective childcare? Food distribution co-ops? Community kitchens? The provision of alternative health care services? Arts and sporting activities for youth and children aimed at indigenizing (decolonizing) our relationships? The list of possible community building activities is endless.

Indigenous activists in my circles are increasingly focused on cultural revival or as Bob Lovelace[85] has put it in his discussions with me

---

[85] Former Co-Chief of the Ardoch Algonquin First Nation, Robert Lovelace is an Elder, educator, author and activist. http://www.aafna.ca/family_council.html

"indigenizing the commons" or "reindigenization". Anishinaabeg activist and scholar Leanne Simpson has stated "I am not so concerned with how we dismantle the master's house… but I am very concerned with how we (re)build our own house. I have spent enough time taking down the master's house and now I want most of my energy to go into visioning and building our new home."[86]

Communities around the globe are increasingly empowering themselves in a variety of ways. Red Cloud Renewable Energy Centre on the Pine Ridge Reservation trains "solar warriors" in the building and maintenance of solar water heaters, solar electric systems, straw bale building, wind breaks, organic gardening and small-scale wind power. In Japan they have created an alternative to cash payments for Elder care called *fureai kipppu* (caring relationship ticket). In this system, which is an alternative to institutionalizing seniors, services such as grocery shopping, escorts, and cooking meals are paid off in the form of credits that can be traded in for services years later or given away to pay the cost of another elderly person's support. This is a system that could be used for a variety of services within a community. Perhaps tickets could be traded for yoga instruction, childcare, house painting, bike repair, driving services or fresh produce from a community garden. Similarly, there are thousands of global communities employing a form of LETS (local exchange trading system). Information and instructions as to how LETS works are available online.

Anyone who doesn't believe these can be radically transformative actions has only to consider, for example, recent lobbying efforts on the part of agribusiness aimed at getting the US government to ban, or at least legislate, backyard gardening. Or consider the fact that the medical establishment, particularly pharmaceutical companies, fights universal coverage for alternative health care, despite evidence of its effectiveness. Consider the flexibility it gives individuals and families when they decrease their dependence on the cash economy. Imagine the quality of relationships and self-empowerment that result from creating, caring for and nurturing rather than destroying, stopping or dismantling something that will be fixed or replaced tomorrow (laws, policies or even windows). Consider the blow it deals to capitalism when people become increasingly independent of an unjust economic system.

I am not naive enough to believe that those in power will ignore us. Sooner or later we will be confronted. Whether we are beaten down, imprisoned and killed (like many activists before us) or we emerge victorious by using community authored tactics and strategies, will in part

---

[86] Simpson, Leanne. *Dancing on Our Turtle's Back: Stories of Nishnaabeg Re-Creation, Resurgence and a New Emergence.* Arbeiter Ring. 2011.

depend on the numbers we represent; the hearts and minds we shift through our work; and the strength and resilience of our communities. Our transformational/revolutionary power lies in role-modeling care, dignity and respect for ourselves and Our Relations.

If we really believe that capitalism is unsustainable then we also must believe it does not require much assistance to collapse. It will collapse under its own weight. We must act with the courage and faith of our convictions. Yes, we must protect life and draw lines in the sand to ensure survival and well being *now*. But what will come after capitalism's collapse if we are not prepared with healthy, sustainable community-based alternatives? Who will create the new and better world if we, who have achieved a level of relational consciousness, don't start acting on our beliefs? Besides, don't these alternatives, in and of themselves, contribute to the demise of a poisonous and violent system?

Personally, I want to be nurturing life when I go down in struggle. I want nurturing life to *be* my struggle.

Activist Self-Care

Having addressed the question of a paradigm shift we can now talk about the implications of that shift for activist self-care. The ways in which this information can be useful to individuals, activists or not, is fairly obvious. At minimum this knowledge would help anyone manage life's stresses better. More importantly, establishing for ourselves an emotional baseline of contentment and satisfaction as well as a healthy sense of compassion can contribute to our personal wellbeing and enhance our relationships, enabling us to extract more joy from our lives.

How will this knowledge help activists specifically? First of all, it suggests strongly that the better we care for ourselves, the more likely we will be in a position to positively impact others. In order to take responsibility for what energies you are radiating, you, first of all want to take responsibility for your own emotional, physical, mental and spiritual wellbeing. You'll want to function at the highest possible level of your spirit. To do this you have to know yourself as well as you possibly can. You have to be as aware as possible of your thoughts and feelings. You have to understand what triggers you into negative or positive states while at the same time offering yourself the same compassion you offer others. You have to treat Our Relations with respect and take responsibility for how your thoughts, words and actions impact them.

There is no guarantee of 100% success in this world. However, you can maximize your chances of effective and loving activist practices by knowing yourself and ensuring that you are acting out of the highest possible motivations. Likewise you can support colleagues in doing the same. Furthermore, everything we can say about self-care also applies to collective-care. When you're in relationship the collective and the self are mutually impacting, inter-dependent and intimately connected.

Collective-Care/Community-Building

Given what the science is saying and how relational wisdoms would have us apply the science, do some of our activities as activists make sense? Do they prevent burnout and enhance wellbeing? Do they help us grow our movements? Do they serve our families, friends and colleagues? Do they role model healthy, sustainable lifeways? Will they build sustainable communities? Will they help us achieve our goals of a socially just world? Will they ensure wellbeing for Our Relations, who in turn take care of us?

These are clearly not yes/no questions. But it's useful to ask them over and over again of our collectives and groups. Reciprocity, wellness and sustainability are key values to think about when doing this work. As this new knowledge can inform our interactions with each other, as well as our relationships to our movements, each of us as individuals *and* collectives should be examining our relationship to our work. We should furthermore not see our work and our lives as being separate and differentiated.

Part of being an activist is choosing to commit to lifting the collective spirit and supporting an upward spiral of responsibility, generosity and appreciation. At the same time, while your own development might be a full time, lifetime job, it makes no sense to do it outside of your relationships with others. Responsibility requires that your actions have to take into account that you are influencing others with your very thoughts/feelings, words and actions and they are doing the same with you. You must understand that, while you cannot control another's reaction to you, you can control yours to them.

Certainly as you recognize inter-connectedness it makes sense to allow this awareness to impact how you interact with your world. This certainly doesn't mean that your course of action will always be clear but it does mean that compassion, generosity and appreciation will increasingly underwrite your interactions. This might make for more meaningful, satisfying and fulfilling relationships all around.

As many discussions I've had over the years confirm, we humans can be cynical and skeptical of human potential and the predisposition to cooperate and collaborate. Certainly, we see evidence of how difficult it can be to work respectfully together. If we as activists, who fervently believe in the value of cooperation and collaboration, can't get it right, what hope does anyone else have?

We can now decide, empowered with various wisdoms as well as the new hard science, to start, if we haven't already, intentionally interacting with each other in ways that are framed with an awareness of our energetic connections. The new science argues in favour of institutions, laws and systems based in compassion, generosity and social justice. If our relationships can transform us as individuals they can transform the collective. And the collective can transform the future. This knowledge has significant implications for social processes and structures.

Our training to be astute social critics encourages us to find flaws and something to critique within every idea, action and vision. We vigorously interrogate all theories to find the gaps, impracticalities and points of disagreement with the philosophies we espouse. Even when we're making progress towards our objectives, some will find and magnify the smallest of imperfections.

Because left wing philosophies hold that social change only comes about through the process of conflict, particularly class conflict, we often feel a compulsion to look for, initiate and heighten tensions, believing that as conflict escalates so does the potential for transformation. As we've seen, some interpretations of these theories, as well as the way people act on them, can leave the most optimistic activist disillusioned, frustrated and resentful. How can we shift a focus on challenging, critiquing and confronting without being dishonest, superficial and insincere about the work we do? Can we acknowledge and pay enough attention to fixing what needs to be fixed while generally maintaining an underlying sense of realistic hopefulness, satisfaction and contentment about our work? How can we be balanced, responsible and accountable yet maintain an overall sense of optimism as we move forward?

Can we be happy revolutionaries? I suppose not if we define happiness as constantly engaging in fun activities and never allowing ourselves to feel angry or sad or discouraged. If we remember that compassion, self-compassion and general optimism promote our collective and individual wellbeing, what are the implications for our work? If we, as individuals, applaud striving for a sense of optimism, positivity and peace within ourselves aren't such aspirations equally worthwhile for our collectives, cooperatives and communities?

There is no one-size-fits-all answer to these questions. However, a friend of mine, a veteran of many years in the feminist, anti-zionist and social justice movements once said to me (and I paraphrase here) that in her Elder years she is tired of focusing on the problems more than the solutions; spending more time trying to find fault than celebrating achievements. More importantly she understands how demoralizing negativity is and, consequently, how it sets the work back. She wants to give more time and attention to what is working well. She wants to focus on energizing, motivating and inspiring people to continue striving for the changes she's been working for all her life.

It's like that old anonymous teaching that crops up on my Facebook page now and again:

An old Cherokee teaches his grandson about life. "A fight is going on inside me," he says to the boy. "It is a terrible fight and it is between two wolves. One is evil - he is anger, envy, sorrow, regret, greed, arrogance, self-pity, guilt, resentment, inferiority, lies, false pride, superiority, and ego.

"The other is good - he is joy, peace, love, hope, serenity, humility, kindness, benevolence, empathy, generosity, truth, compassion, and faith. The same fight is going on inside you - and inside every other person, too."

The grandson thinks about it for a minute and then asks, "Which wolf will win?"

The old Cherokee simply replies, "The one you feed." [87]

Similarly, the world we co-create will be the one we collectively feed.

Inherited Struggles

I sometimes ask participants in my workshops to draw pictures or write words on a common writing surface that, in some way, relate to their vision of social justice. I have been disappointed in *some* of the responses. Examples of the more disappointing depictions include burning government buildings, police barricades coming down and uniformed authorities on the run from "the masses". Inverse triangles with white folks at the bottom of a hierarchy where people of colour rule is another image I've seen people jokingly create. I think when I get this type of response to an "envision social justice" exercise, it reflects several facts: 1) some folks are more focused on "the struggle" than the ultimate goal, 2) some people believe that the process of struggle is somehow irrelevant to what we achieve in the end and 3) individual rage, anger and fear makes it difficult to invoke creativity and imagination around the world we're working hard to create. These are not the depictions of struggle I want to hand down to the upcoming generations.

---

[87] First People American Indian Legends website: http://www.firstpeople.us/FP-Html-Legends/TwoWolves-Cherokee.html

If we consider ourselves as social justice activists to be healers of collectives, communities and society perhaps our training should include self-healing at an individual as well as collective level. Besides evaluating how close we are getting to our social justice goals, we might also interrogate how the work is transforming us. Capitalism, colonialism and hetero-patriarchy make us sick. Are our responses healing us? Are our actions generating wellbeing for others? Or are we, unintentionally reproducing the kind of relationships that made us sick in the first place?

In answering these questions it's easy to point to the barriers, challenges and power that is blocking our path to wellness. However, as we very well know, the journey in and of itself can be healing. If we don't make it to the mountaintop there is still plenty to enjoy on the way up, especially if we ensure that those who follow have a clearer, easier path than we did. That realization alone is satisfying, healing and contributes to the ultimate goal.

As the one of my songs, *Inherited Struggles*, goes:

Verse 1:
Together we celebrate
Rising warrior might
Respect and honour
Simply the truth of light

Chorus A:
Inherited struggles
Passed down through the ages
Eternal riddles
We lament nothing changes

And yet, and yet

Challenge evolves spirit
Moves us beyond fear
Grief merely ignites
The passions that we feel

Verse 2
Longings for justice and peace are
Bequeathed to our children
Lessons in giving absorbed by
The next generation

Chorus A

Bridge:
Lives of joy have purpose
Short or long
Fighting for justice
Keeps us strong

Chorus B:
Inherited struggles
Passed down through the ages
Eternal riddles
We lament nothing changes

We will remember
We will remember

Challenge evolves spirit
Moves us beyond fear
Grief merely ignites
The passions that we feel[88]

Social justice is not utopia. Social justice is not stagnant. Activism
is not about struggling for a world where no problems or challenges exist;
otherwise we wouldn't experience spiritual growth and might as well be
dead. Perhaps social justice is a kind of social homeostasis where we
collectively and continuously shift and transform to respond to each other,
Our Relations and life in general in an effort to maintain wellbeing for all.
Social justice conceived of as a continuously shifting point might provide us
with the flexibility to evolve, create and get the most out of our life
experiences. Perhaps this concept of social justice allows us to experience a
sense of oneness with Beinghood/the Great Spirit; to feel the joys of
existing, sharing and contributing to the kind of wellness that ensures the
ongoing evolution and regeneration of life.

Maybe social justice isn't about arriving; maybe it's about the
journey and how we take care of each other along the way. Just as healers
help individuals achieve wellness, maybe we can consider ourselves as
activists to be "social healers".

---

[88] Lyrics here are reordered from the performance and recorded versions to
facilitate reading.

ABOUT THE AUTHOR

Author, singer/songwriter and community activist **Zainab Amadahy**
is of African American, Cherokee (Tsalagi) and European descent.
Based in Toronto, she likes to describe herself as an "Indigenous settler".

You can find more of Zainab's writings, including free downloads, at
www.swallowsongs.com.

Made in the USA
San Bernardino, CA
07 September 2016